EXPLORE *the* BIBLE

ADULT COMMENTARY

ACTS
(Part 2)

Sharon H. Gritz

WINTER 2000-2001

Volume 5, Number 2

LifeWay®
Christian Resources

ADULT COMMENTARY

PRODUCTION TEAM

Tom Hudson
Biblical Studies Designer

Angela L. Brown
Graphic Designer

Melissa Finn
Technical Specialist

Angelyn Golmon
Production Specialist

Ross H. McLaren
Biblical Studies Specialist

Judith A. Wooldridge
Senior Product Development Specialist

MANAGEMENT PERSONNEL

Michael Felder, Manager
Adult VBS-Ventures Section

Rick Edwards, Director
Adult Sunday School Ministry Department

Louis Hanks, Associate Director
Sunday School Group

Bill L. Taylor, Director
Sunday School Group

MINISTRY SERVICES PERSONNEL

John McClendon
Consultant

Richard E. Dodge
Ministry Consultant

Alan Raughton
Manager

Send questions/comments to
Tom Hudson
LifeWay Christian Resources,
127 Ninth Avenue
North, Nashville, TN 37234-0175
or send email to **aetb@lifeway.com**

About the Cover
Exterior of the Mamertinum Prison in Rome where it is believed Paul was a prisoner.

Explore the Bible: Adult Commentary (ISSN 0164-4440) is published quarterly by LifeWay Christian Resources of the Southern Baptist Convention, 127 Ninth Avenue, North, Nashville, Tennessee 37234: Gene Mims, President, LifeWay Church Resources, a division of LifeWay Christian Resources of the Southern Baptist Convention; James T. Draper, Jr., President, and Ted Warren, Executive Vice President, LifeWay Christian Resources; Bill L. Taylor, Director, Sunday School Group. Printed in the U.S.A. © Copyright 2000, LifeWay Christian Resources of the Southern Baptist Convention. All rights reserved.

If you need help with an order, WRITE LifeWay Church Resources Customer Service, 127 Ninth Avenue, North, Nashville, TN 37234-0113; FAX (615) 251-5933; EMAIL to CustomerService@lifeway.com; or PHONE 1-800-458-2772. Mail address changes to: *Explore the Bible: Adult Commentary*, LifeWay Church Resources Customer Service, 127 Ninth Avenue, North, Nashville, TN 37234-0113.

This periodical is designed for all adults using the Explore the Bible Series. We believe the Bible has God for its author, salvation for its end, and truth, without any mixture of error, for its matter. The 1998 statement of *The Baptist Faith and Message* is our doctrinal guideline.

Scripture taken from the Holy Bible, *New International Version*, copyright © 1973, 1978, 1984 by International Bible Society.

ADULT COMMENTARY

IN THIS ISSUE

*Christmas Lesson
**Sanctity of Human Life Lesson

INTRODUCING

ACTS: THE MODEL FOR THE CHURCH
OF THE 21ST CENTURY

The Book of Acts begins the wonderful story of the triumph of the Christian gospel. The story centers on the gospel and human witnesses. The gospel is powerful. In Acts the gospel triumphs over political opposition, religious jealousy, pagan misunderstandings, social barriers, racial differences, and geographical boundaries. Acts is the story of faithful witnesses led and empowered by the Holy Spirit to tell the good news wherever they went. This combination of a powerful gospel and faithful witnesses is the model for the church in the 21st century.

Distinctive Features

Several features make Acts unique in the New Testament. It is a transitional book, bridging the Gospels and the Letters, particularly Paul's letters. While the Gospels tell the origin of the gospel, Acts describes its progress in the first-century world. When the Gospels conclude, the overwhelming majority of Jesus' followers were believing Jews. The Letters are addressed to churches composed primarily of believing Gentiles. Acts describes the transition from a Jewish majority to a Gentile majority. Acts opens with Jewish believers in Jerusalem and closes with a Gentile church in Rome.

Acts is the second of a two-volume work. Comparing Luke 1:3 and Acts 1:1 leads to the conclusion that the same writer produced two books, both dedicated or directed to a person named Theophilus. The evidence points strongly to Luke as the God-inspired author of both volumes. These two books are the only New Testament books written by a Gentile.

Acts uniquely furnishes the historical background for Paul's life and ministry, though it is not intended as a biography of Paul. Acts describes the planting of Christian congregations between Jerusalem and Rome. Attempts to reconstruct the historical setting of church life in the first century from only the letters have not been satisfying. Acts supplies much information that cannot be gleaned from any other source.

Purposes

Students of Acts find several possible purposes behind its writing. To discern these, a logical beginning point is to look at what Luke revealed in his opening words to Theophilus. The stated purpose of the Gospel of Luke is to confirm and apparently to complete for Theophilus the things he had been taught (Luke 1:4) by presenting a complete and orderly account of the good news about Jesus Christ. Acts continues that same general purpose of establishing Theophilus in the Christian faith.

Many see the basic theme and specific purpose of the Book of Acts in Acts 1:8, namely, that Acts was written to record the geographical expansion of Christianity: from Jerusalem (1—7), to Judea, Samaria, and other regions (8—12), and to the wider world (13—28).

Acts also presents both the unity and the universality of the Christian faith. It explains how the early church spanned diverse religious, racial, and national boundaries. Acts witnesses to the gospel as the one way to God for all people—Jews, Samaritans, and Gentiles. Acts belabors the point that there was not a Jewish gospel, a Samaritan gospel, and a Gentile gospel. The book insists that the gospel of Christ is the one and only way to salvation for all the people of the earth.

The Book of Acts also shows Christianity was not a political threat to the Roman Empire. Acts presents the Christian message as rooted in the Person and work of Christ through the Holy Spirit and shows it to be at heart a spiritual movement. Government officials usually appear in Acts as somewhat tolerant, if not favorable, to Christianity, but certainly not antagonistic to it.

Structure

Acts falls quite naturally into two major sections: the activity of the Jerusalem church in chapters 1—12 and the journeys of Paul in chapters 13—28. The first major section describes the early church in Jerusalem (chaps. 1—7) and its expansion into surrounding regions (chaps. 8—12). The first two chapters of Acts preserve the account of the Holy Spirit's empowerment of the Jerusalem church for the purpose of being Christ's witness. Acts 3—5 tells about the church's Spirit-empowered witness among the Jews of Jerusalem. One emphasis is the rapid expansion of the church in Jerusalem by means of large numbers of people responding to the gospel (2:41,47; 4:4; 5:14).

The Jerusalem church took its witness into adjoining areas. Stephen, Philip, and Peter led this outreach effort. At the cost of his life, Stephen insisted that the gospel was not only for Jews but also for Gentiles (chaps. 6—7). Philip, a lay member of the early church, took the gospel into Samaria, then offered it to an Ethiopian as directed by the Holy Spirit (chap. 8). (Saul's conversion is reported in 9:1-31.) Peter preached and performed some notable miracles in several coastal towns (9:32-43). He obeyed the Spirit's direction to take the gospel to Cornelius, a Gentile of Caesarea (10:1—11:18). Christians who had scattered from Jerusalem because of persecution established a predominantly Gentile church at Antioch in Syria (11:19-30). Antioch became the primary church base from which the missionary outreach to regions beyond was launched. Acts 12 takes the narrative back to Jerusalem to describe how the church there endured persecution.

The second major section of Acts describes three of Paul's major church planting missions (13:1—21:16), followed by his witness through arrest and imprisonment (21:17—28:31). The church at Antioch commissioned Paul and Barnabas for a mission to Gentiles (chaps. 13—14). At the conclusion of the mission they joined others at a major church conference in Jerusalem to defend the full acceptance into the church of believing Gentiles (15:1-35). After Paul and Barnabas parted ways, Acts traces two additional missionary journeys of Paul, with an intervening trip back to Antioch to report his labors (15:36—21:16).

Acts concludes by recounting Paul's arrest in Jerusalem and imprisonments in Caesarea and Rome (21:17—28:31). While the messenger was imprisoned, the message was not bound. Paul bore faithful witness to kings, rulers, and other authorities. Acts includes a detailed account of Paul's transfer by ship from Caesarea to Rome, a transfer made because he had appealed his case to Caesar. The book ends with Paul's case pending before the emperor but with the Christian message continuing to go forth.

Writer and Date of Writing

The close connection between the opening verses of the Gospel of Luke and the Book of Acts leads to the conclusion that the same God-inspired person wrote both. Longstanding, strong tradition holds that writer to have been Luke, who dedicated both volumes to the same person, Theophilus (Luke 1:3; Acts 1:1). Students of both volumes often note their similarities of style and vocabulary. Luke joined the two books by the common link of Jesus' ascension—the Gospel of Luke ends with the ascension and Acts begins with it.

Sections of Acts are written in the first person (usually termed the "we sections"), suggesting the writer was present on those occasions. A comparison of Paul's traveling companions at the times and places of the "we sections" narrows the possible writers to Luke, who can be demonstrated to have been present on all these occasions. Those occasions are Paul's travel from Troas to Philippi (16:10-12), his journey from Philippi to Jerusalem (20:6—21:17), and his voyage from Caesarea to Rome (27:1—28:16).

Luke is mentioned by name only three times in the New Testament. Each occurrence is in one of Paul's letters where he sent greetings from his associates. The reference in Colossians 4:14 tells that Luke was a physician and suggests by implication that he was a Gentile. (In the greeting Paul seems to distinguish his Jewish associates from his non-Jewish companions; Luke is mentioned in the second category.) Paul mentioned Luke in Philemon 24 but gave no further details about him, only calling him a fellow worker. In 2 Timothy 4:11 Paul lamented that only Luke was with him, his other associates having moved on to minister in other places or else having deserted him. Luke's having been a physician is somewhat confirmed by much medical terminology in both volumes. However, that terminology would probably also have been known and used by informed nonmedical people.

Older tradition holds that Luke came originally from Antioch, the place where Paul's missionary journeys began. More recent opinion holds that Luke probably hailed from either Macedonia or Antioch in Pisidia.

Two major opinions exist about the date when Luke wrote Acts. The early view suggests Luke wrote Acts before A.D. 64. This view is connected with the last chapter of Acts, which ends with Paul still a prisoner in Rome. This view accounts for the rather abrupt ending of Acts by claiming it was written during the two-year period Paul remained a prisoner in Rome.

The later view holds a date of A.D. 70-80. Luke wrote his Gospel before he wrote Acts, and the Gospel's content shows that the Gospel of Mark was one of the sources Luke carefully investigated before writing his own Gospel (Luke 1:1-3). The Gospel of Mark was probably written after A.D. 65 and the events of Acts 28. While neither the earlier nor later date can be proved beyond doubt, opinion leans toward the decade of the 70's.

ADULT EXPLORE THE BIBLE SERIES
STUDY PLAN*

	FALL	WINTER	SPRING	SUMMER
2000-2001	Acts 1:1—15:35 (The Model for the Church of the 21st Century)	Acts 15:36—28:31	Ruth, 1 Samuel (Faith in Crises)	Amos, Hosea (Passion for Right Living)
2001-2002	1 & 2 Thessalonians (Living the Faith)	Deuteronomy (A Covenant People)	Ephesians (God's New People)	2 Samuel (1 Chronicles) (David: Lessons on Faith and Frailty)
2002-2003	John 1—12	John 13—21 (New Life)	1 Kings (1 Chron. 29— 2 Chron. 21) (Stay Focused on the Lord)	Galatians, James (Freedom for Responsible Living)

*Each Fall quarter this chart will be updated to reveal an additional year of the study plan.

The Week of December 3

CONSISTENT WITNESSING

Background Passage: Acts 15:36—16:40
Lesson Passages: Acts 16:9-15,25-33

INTRODUCTION

One of my college professors required students to keep a journal of observations on class discussions. My efforts to view things from a Christian perspective were reflected in my journal. After class one day, the instructor asked if he could walk me to my dorm. He had been reading my assigned journal entries, and these had raised questions in his mind. He brought up my faith and how important it seemed in my life. God had provided me with a witnessing opportunity.

This lesson focuses on Paul's missionary call to Macedonia and his responsiveness to witnessing opportunities that resulted in the conversions of Lydia, a Philippian jailer, and their households. Paul maintained his faithfulness in witnessing regardless of his circumstances. We too can become alert and responsive to witnessing opportunities in our lives.

Acts 15:36—16:40

1. Paul and Barnabas Disagreed (15:36-38)
2. Silas Joined Paul (15:39-41)
3. Timothy Joined the Missionary Team (16:1-5)
4. Paul Was Called to Macedonia (16:6-10)
5. Paul Witnessed in Philippi (16:11-40)

THE BACKGROUND

The Jerusalem conference (Acts 15) not only affirmed Paul's work on his first missionary journey but also laid the foundation for his second. The conference resolved a conflict that Paul's work had created—a conflict over what is required of Gentiles for salvation. The leaders of the Jerusalem church agreed that Gentiles were not required to be circumcised or follow other ritualistic rules of Judaism to become Christians. For practical reasons, however, they did request that Gentile believers refrain from practices that would strain their relationships with Jewish Christians.

Deciding this issue prepared the way for great progress in missions.

With the controversy resolved, Paul and Barnabas once more devoted their energies to evangelism and discipleship, eventually deciding to begin a second missionary trip.The apostles purposed to visit the churches previously established to see how they were doing, but God had different and larger plans. This journey would take the gospel from the eastern Mediterranean cities of Jerusalem and Antioch to the Greek cities of Philippi, Thessalonica, Athens, and Corinth. Much more extensive than the first, this missionary journey spanned a period of three or four years (A.D. 49-52). On it, Paul would continue his missionary strategy of preaching first in the Jewish synagogues, planting churches in cities, and remaining sensitive to the differing cultural contexts of his witness.

THE LESSON PASSAGE

1. Paul and Barnabas Disagreed (Acts 15:36-38)

In the days following the Jerusalem Conference Paul and Barnabas continued to teach and preach in Antioch. Paul's concern for the churches they had founded on the first missionary journey led him to propose to Barnabas a return visit. Barnabas agreed and wanted to take John Mark, his cousin, with them again. Paul refused to start a second journey with this young man who had abandoned them on their first mission. Another source of tension between Paul and Barnabas could have come from an incident that took place in Antioch, evidently after the Jerusalem conference (Gal. 2:11-13). Peter and Barnabas gave in to pressure from some Jewish believers from Jerusalem and stopped eating with Gentiles. Paul sharply confronted Peter. Barnabas, who followed Peter's example, also experienced Paul's displeasure.

2. Silas Joined Paul (Acts 15:39-41)

The intense disagreement between Paul and Barnabas about Mark caused them to break up their missionary partnership and go separate ways. Barnabas took Mark and went to Cyprus. (Paul eventually became reconciled to Mark and trusted him as a coworker, Col. 4:10; 2 Tim. 4:11; Philem. 24.) Paul chose Silas as his partner in ministry for his second missionary effort. Silas was one of the two Jerusalem delegates formerly sent to Antioch (Acts 15:22) and was a Roman citizen, as was Paul. The two men strengthened the churches in Syria and Cilicia.

3. Timothy Joined the Missionary Team (Acts 16:1-5)

In Lystra Paul took special notice of a disciple named Timothy, a young man highly esteemed by other believers in the area, and decided to have Timothy join the mission team. As the son of a Jewish mother and Greek father, Jews considered Timothy to be Jewish. His mother and grandmother had instructed him in the Jewish faith and Scriptures. Paul circumcised him to avoid any hindrance to his witness in Jewish communities on the tour. Following Timothy's circumcision, the missionary team continued on its way through the Galatian cities, visiting churches established on the first journey. Everywhere they visited, they delivered the decrees set forth at the Jerusalem conference. This strengthened the churches in the faith and caused their numbers to increase daily.

4. Paul Was Called to Macedonia (Acts 16:6-10)

Paul, Silas, and Timothy headed into northern Phrygia and then evidently moved eastward into northern Galatia. The Holy Spirit, however, forbade them to enter the Roman province of Asia. The missionaries traveled north to Mysia. When they tried to enter Bithynia, the Spirit of Jesus stopped them again. The missionary group then followed a course between Asia and Bithynia, eventually reaching Troas. Its artificial harbor provided the main sea access to Macedonia. From Troas Paul might have sailed in several directions, but God directed his path.

Verse 9: *During the night Paul had a vision of a man of Macedonia standing and begging him, "Come over to Macedonia and help us."*

After guiding Paul negatively with a series of "closed doors," God gave Paul positive direction through a *vision* at *night*. A *man of Macedonia* appeared to him, *begging him* to *come over to Macedonia and help* the people there. The man's request clearly indicated his nationality.

Verse 10: *After Paul had seen the vision, we got ready at once to leave for Macedonia, concluding that God had called us to preach the gospel to them.*

Paul and his companions understood his vision was God's call to take the *gospel* to Macedonia. They responded *at once,* following the Lord's direction without hesitation. They found passage on a ship sailing for Neapolis. Though Paul might first have planned to evangelize the eastern shore of the Aegean Sea, God directed him to its western shore where Paul planted the gospel in Philippi, Thessalonica, and Corinth. On his third missionary journey he would work on the eastern shore, staying in Ephesus. Paul's following God's guidance took the gospel westward. Ultimately, Europe and the Western world were evangelized.

At Troas the first of the "we" sections of Acts appears (16:10-17; 20:5-15; 21:1-18; 27:1—28:16). *We got ready* indicates that Luke joined the missionary team at this time. As the narrator, he recorded his own part in the story. The team now numbered four: Paul, Silas, Timothy, and Luke.

Paul and his associates responded immediately to God's call to preach the gospel in Macedonia. We too should respond readily when God presents us with a witnessing opportunity. Let us pray that God's Spirit will make us sensitive and alert to such opportunities.

5. Paul Witnessed in Philippi (Acts 16:11-40)

Luke devoted more space to the mission in Philippi than to any other city on Paul's second and third missionary journeys—even though the apostle had only a brief stay there. The visit to Philippi illustrated the difficulty the Christian mission had in a Roman environment, especially where the gospel affected the beliefs and economic interests of the local people. Nevertheless, Paul's efforts led to the establishment of a Christian church there.

Verse 11: *From Troas we put out to sea and sailed straight for Samothrace, and the next day on to Neapolis.*

Good weather and favorable winds enabled their ship to reach **Samothrace** the first day. *Samothrace* is a mountainous island in the northeastern part of the Aegean Sea. It lay on a direct line between Troas and Neapolis. The island became a stopover for ships plying their trade in the North Aegean because captains preferred to anchor there rather than face the hazards of the sea at night.

Paul and his three friends probably stayed overnight on the island. The **next day** they arrived by ship at **Neapolis** on the Macedonian coast. Since Luke, the narrator, traveled with the group, he provided a port-by-port description of the voyage with specific mention of the time it took. The wind at this crossing must have favored the travelers, for it took only two days to sail the distance. The reverse journey from Neapolis to Troas took five days (20:6). Neapolis was the port for the commercial center of Philippi, which lay 10 miles further inland. Neapolis was on the Via Egnatia, an important military road carrying commercial goods from the Adriatic to the Aegean Sea.

Verse 12: *From there we traveled to Philippi, a Roman colony and the leading city of that district of Macedonia. And we stayed there several days.*

Disembarking at Neapolis, the missionary group **traveled** northwest **to Philippi.** *Philippi* was on a plain bounded by mountains to the north and northeast, with the rivers Strymon and Nestos on either side. Shielded from the sea by a rocky ridge, it lay astride the Via Egnatia and near the Gangites River, a tributary of the Strymon. This city received its name from Philip of Macedon, the father of Alexander the Great, who seized the gold mines in the vicinity and fortified what had formerly been the Thasian settlement of Krenides. In 356 B.C. he established a large Greek colony there. With the rest of Macedonia, Philippi passed under Roman control in 168 B.C. In 146 B.C. Rome included it within the reorganized province of Macedonia, whose capital was at Thessalonica. Shortly thereafter it was connected to other important Roman cities by the Via Egnatia.

During Roman times, the fame of Philippi derived from its having been the site of the decisive battle of the second civil war in 42 B.C., where Mark Anthony and Octavian (later called Augustus) defeated Brutus and Cassius. After the war the victors settled many Roman army veterans at Philippi. After defeating Anthony and Cleopatra at the battle of Actium in 31 B.C., Octavian granted the city the status of a **Roman colony** and settled more military veterans there. A *colony* possessed the rights of self-government under Roman laws and freedom from taxes. Macedonia was an unusual Roman province because it was divided into four administrative subprovinces. Philippi belonged to the first district, but that district's capital city was Amphipolis. Luke's expression **the leading city of that district of Macedonia** might have meant a city of the first district of Macedonia. Or Luke might have reflected a local claim that Philippi was Macedonia's foremost city, or he could have been expressing his own opinion of the city. Philippi had importance during the New Testament period because of its agriculture, its strategic commercial location on both sea and land routes, its gold mines, and its status as a Roman colony. It also had a famous school of medicine.

Verse 13: *On the Sabbath we went outside the city gate to the river, where we expected to find a place of prayer. We sat down and began to speak to the women who had gathered there.*

When Paul visited a new city, he typically attended the local Jewish synagogue on the first Sabbath after his arrival to make the Christian message known to the Jews first. Consequently, Paul, Silas, Timothy, and Luke evidently set themselves up in the city waiting for the next **Sabbath** before beginning their witness. **Expected to find** indicates that Paul and his companions did not know for certain where the Jews met and that they had not been lodging with Jews. They depended on what vague information they could pick up from the local people. So they **went outside the city gate to the river . . . to find a place of prayer.** In Jewish law only men made up the congregation. Wherever there were 10 male heads of households who could attend regularly, these 10 men could form a synagogue. Failing this, Jewish worshipers could arrange a place of prayer under the open sky and near a river or sea, though rabbinical sources did not explicitly say it must be by water. The proximity to water would have allowed for Jewish ritual purification. Philippi apparently did not have the quorum of men needed, so it had no synagogue. No number of women could compensate for the absence of even one man.

On the Sabbath, therefore, the four missionaries walked outside the city in search of a Jewish *place of prayer.* They probably headed toward the Gangites River about a mile and a quarter west of the city. There they found some **women who had gathered.** This place of prayer was simply a place where the women gathered by custom to pray. It was probably outside the town because the authorities would not allow the Jews to meet inside the town limits or because there was no formally constituted synagogue. These women, Jewish and God-fearing Gentiles, went through the appointed Jewish service of prayer for the Sabbath Day, even if they could not constitute a regular synagogue congregation. A synagogue service included, if possible, an exposition or exhortation and blessing from a traveling Jewish teacher. Paul and his associates assumed this role. They *sat down,* taking the usual posture a speaker assumed in a synagogue, and addressed the women. They told them the story of Jesus.

Verse 14: *One of those listening was a woman named Lydia, a dealer in purple cloth from the city of Thyatira, who was a worshiper of God. The Lord opened her heart to respond to Paul's message.*

Among the women gathered there *listening* to Paul, one stood out— **Lydia.** She was from **Thyatira,** a city of western Asia Minor. Thyatira was in the ancient kingdom of Lydia before its incorporation into the Roman province of Asia, and it continued to be considered in Lydia. Therefore, the woman's being called *Lydia* perhaps meant simply the Lydian lady. Luke described her as a **dealer in purple cloth.** Thyatira was famous as a center for making purple dyes and for dyeing clothes. Women carried out this industry primarily in their homes. Lydia had come to Philippi as a trader. Purple goods were expensive and often associated with royalty. Thus, her business brought her much income. Lydia's invitation to the four missionaries to stay in her home indicates that she had guest rooms and servants to accommodate their needs adequately.

Lydia was a **worshiper of God.** She was a devout Gentile who, like Cornelius, believed in God but had not become a full convert to Judaism. Thyatira had a large Jewish community. Perhaps Lydia had first come to her faith in the one true God there. She carried her interest in Judaism with her to Philippi. The fact that Lydia, a woman, was engaged in business strongly suggests that she was single or widowed. Some of the women gathered for worship were probably relatives and servants living in her home. As Lydia listened, **the Lord opened her heart to respond to Paul's message.** Luke emphasized that her conversion resulted from the action of God who opens the heart, that is, the mind, to receive His word. This did not take away her responsibility to repent and believe the gospel. She responded to the Lord in faith, acknowledging Jesus as Lord.

Of all the churches Paul founded, the Philippian congregation stands out for their warm relationship with Paul and their generosity toward him.

This church sent support for his missionary efforts in other places (Phil. 4:15-18; 2 Cor. 11:8-9). Perhaps Lydia served as a principal contributor and encouraged this ministry to Paul. The prominence of women such as Lydia in Paul's missionary work is reported in Acts, including those of Thessalonica (17:4) and Berea (17:12), as well as Damaris in Athens (17:34) and Priscilla in Corinth (18:1-4). The more elevated status of women in Greek and Roman society of that day, as indicated by their legal privileges, allowed this participation.

Verse 15: *When she and the members of her household were baptized, she invited us to her home. "If you consider me a believer in the Lord," she said, "come and stay at my house." And she persuaded us.*

After the baptism of Lydia and the **members of her household,** she urged the missionary party to stay at her home. Lydia made their acceptance of her offer of hospitality the test of whether these ministers really believed she had become a believer. She wanted to give practical proof of her conversion. ***She persuaded*** them, and they did become her guests. Lydia opened her home to the missionaries and allowed her home to become the gathering place for the entire Christian community (16:40). She shared her material goods with others, particularly with those who ministered the gospel.

Lydia shared her faith as well. As leader of her household, she led them to join her in faith and baptism. The *members of her household* included servants and/or dependents who lived with her. Baptism symbolized the outward expression of the salvation that Lydia and the members of her household received and the faith they demonstrated. The act of baptism identified them with the Christian community.

As new people enter our lives and we develop relationships with them, we can look for opportunities to invite them to repent and receive Jesus Christ. What kind of invitations are we extending?

While continuing their ministry in Philippi, the missionary team found themselves followed and troubled by a demon-possessed servant girl (16:16-17). Paul healed the girl by commanding in the name of Jesus Christ that the spirit come out of her. In so doing, he removed the slave girl's masters' source of income—the girl had been used as a fortune teller. Her owners dragged Paul and Silas before the civil authorities. Their charges appealed to the anti-Jewish feelings and nationalistic Roman pride of the crowd (16:20-21). The magistrates had the two men flogged and jailed without serious investigation of the charges against them. As Roman citizens, Paul and Silas were politically exempt from such treatment; but the frenzy of the mob and the carelessness of the magistrates prevailed.

The jailer, probably a retired soldier, fastened the missionaries' legs in stocks in the most secure part of the prison (16:24). Stocks often had more than two holes for the legs, enabling prisoners' legs to be forced wide apart so as to cause cramping pain. The jailer did not care for his prisoners' comfort but wanted to make sure they did not escape. Perhaps the jailer took extreme precautions because he feared Paul and Silas, who had displayed unusual powers.

Verse 25: *About midnight Paul and Silas were praying and singing hymns to God, and the other prisoners were listening to them.*

The missionaries would have had difficulty sleeping that night because of the pain from their flogging and their uncomfortable positions. After such brutal treatment, Paul and Silas easily could have complained of their situation. *About midnight* the **other prisoners** heard sounds coming from the missionaries' part of the jail—not groans and curses but prayers and hymns. In the midst of their suffering Paul and Silas displayed their trust in God and their joy *by praying and singing hymns* of praise to Him. The prayers offered might have been simply of praise to God. Luke did not suggest that they prayed for release. Their behavior was a positive witness about God before the other prisoners.

Verse 26: *Suddenly there was such a violent earthquake that the foundations of the prison were shaken. At once all the prison doors flew open, and everybody's chains came loose.*

The area around Philippi often experiences earthquakes and tremors. The timing and effects of this one made it a miracle. The **earthquake** caused the **prison doors** to spring open and the prisoners' **chains** to come **loose.** Was this God's response to the joyful confessions by the missionaries? Escape became possible even though the prisoners probably had fetters attached to their arms or legs. Perhaps Paul and Silas's behavior influenced them, keeping them from running away.

Verse 27: *The jailer woke up, and when he saw the prison doors open, he drew his sword and was about to kill himself because he thought the prisoners had escaped.*

The earthquake *woke up* the jailer. Immediately he went to investigate the damage. The worst had happened: the *prison doors* were *open.* He assumed the prisoners had escaped. In Roman law a guard who allowed his prisoner to escape was liable to the same penalty the prisoner would have suffered. This jailer's former training as a soldier emphasized the military ideas of duty and discipline. He saw only one course open to himself— suicide. He preferred death by his own hand than by Roman justice.

Verse 28: *But Paul shouted, "Don't harm yourself! We are all here!"*

While the jailer could see nothing as he looked into the darkness of the prison, those within could probably see his figure outlined in the doorway. They could see what he was about to do. As he stood there about to drive his sword into his throat or heart, **Paul shouted** for him to stop, assuring him they were *all* still in the jail. Not only were Paul and Silas still there, but also they apparently had kept the other prisoners from leaving.

Verse 29: *The jailer called for lights, rushed in and fell trembling before Paul and Silas.*

Since it was midnight, the jailer called for **lights** to dispel the darkness of the prison. Rushing in, he *fell trembling before Paul and Silas.* He went straight to the two missionaries, perhaps regarding them as the cause of the earthquake. The whole incident with the slave girl might have led him to believe they were some kind of divine messengers. Paul did not object to the jailor's falling before them, indicating that he understood the man's posture as one of respect and submission, not of worship.

Verse 30: *He then brought them out and asked, "Sirs, what must I do to be saved?"*

Sirs, literally *lords,* carries a note of respect and perhaps adoration here. With his shout Paul had saved the jailor's life. The God Paul served had defeated all the man's efforts at prison security. Such a God deserved respect.

Something about these two men convinced the jailer they would have the answer to his question. Perhaps he had heard the servant girl shouting that Paul spoke of the way of salvation (16:17). Maybe he even had heard the missionaries preach or had received reports of their message. He might have recalled the words of Paul and Silas's hymns. He realized he had to come to terms with the God these two proclaimed. His question showed he recognized his spiritual need. It opened the way for the two missionaries to give him the good news about Jesus Christ. Everyone who comes to faith must ask in some fashion, "What must I do to be saved?"

Verse 31: *They replied, "Believe in the Lord Jesus, and you will be saved—you and your household."*

Paul's response reflected the early Christian confessional statement, *Jesus is Lord.* Paul emphasized the necessity of trusting in **Jesus** as **Lord.** Jesus is Savior to those to whom He is *Lord.* The apostle offered the gift of salvation to the jailer and his **whole household.** These family members, however, had to hear the word and believe for themselves.

Verse 32: *Then they spoke the word of the Lord to him and to all the others in his house.*

All the others in his house were present when Paul and Silas shared the gospel. The missionaries provided a fuller explanation of the gospel message than the brief answer Paul had given to the jailer's question (16:31). The whole family heard the gospel and came to faith in Christ. Since they came from a pagan background, their new faith had two aspects—faith in Jesus as Savior and faith in God as the one true God. For Paul and Silas, sharing the gospel message took priority over treatment for the wounds caused by their earlier beating.

Verse 33: *At that hour of the night the jailer took them and washed* *their wounds; then immediately he and all his family were baptized.*

To judge by their actions, the jailer and his household truly believed in Christ. The jailer revealed his change of heart by caring for the physical needs of the missionaries. He did what he could to lessen the effects of their beating the previous day. He bathed the **wounds** of Paul and Silas, probably at a well in the prison courtyard where the household water supply would be located. Then the missionaries **baptized** him and his family. Although Paul and Silas had put the preaching of the gospel before their personal comfort, the jailer saw to their needs before being baptized.

The jailer further showed his care for the prisoners by taking them into his house, where he provided for them a meal (16:34). This expressed Christian fellowship and hospitality as well as joy and gratitude for his and his family's conversion. He no longer saw Paul and Silas as prisoners; he saw them as brothers in Christ. After the meal the missionaries presumably had to return to their places in the prison. They probably considered the pain of the flogging and the stocks well worth the salvation and joy that were brought into the Philippian jailer's home that night.

At daylight the magistrates sent the order for the release of Paul and Silas (16:35). Paul identified himself as a Roman citizen, however, and insisted on an official apology. To beat and imprison a Roman citizen without a trial was a serious offense. The magistrates came, apologized for their illegal actions, and personally escorted the two men out of prison. The officials asked the men to leave Philippi, likely wanting to avoid further embarrassment or opposition from the crowd. Paul might have insisted on the public apology from the officials in order to head off trouble for the Christians. He wanted believers to have a good reputation with the authorities. Luke clearly showed that Christians had broken no Roman laws.

The missionaries then visited the Christians of the city at Lydia's house. They encouraged the believers before departing for the next city.

How do we respond to difficulties caused by our Christian witness and example? Paul and Silas provide us a challenging example. They maintained their faith and were consistent witnesses. Let us witness by example at all times and be ready to tell others how they can be saved.

FOR FURTHER STUDY

1. Read the articles "Lydia of Thyatira" and "The Second Missionary Journey" in the Winter issue of *Biblical Illustrator*.

2. See the detailed map of Paul's second missionary journey in *Holman Bible Atlas*, page 246.

3. Read the article on "Philippi" in the *Holman Bible Dictionary*, page 1105.

4. Read "The Importance of Roman Citizenship" in the Summer 1993 issue of *Biblical Illustrator*.

The Week of December 10

WISE WITNESSING

Background Passage: Acts 17:1-34
Lesson Passages: Acts 17:16,22-34

INTRODUCTION

One summer I worked with a small group of seminary students in a church-planting effort in Mexico near the Rio Grande. Before we began our ministry, we had several orientation sessions on the customs and religious beliefs of the people who lived in that area. We needed to understand them so we could share the gospel with them more effectively.

This lesson focuses on Paul's preaching the gospel in Athens. The apostle showed wisdom in using terms familiar to the Athenians as he explained the Christian message. His example challenges us to plan how we may witness more wisely to particular persons.

Acts 17:1-34

1. Paul's Witness to the Thessalonians (17:1-4)
2. The Jews' Opposition to Paul (17:5-9)
3. Paul's Witness to the Bereans (17:10-12)
4. Paul's Flight to Athens (17:13-15)
5. Paul's Witness to the Athenians (17:16-34)

THE BACKGROUND

Paul and his companions continued the second missionary journey by moving to Thessalonica. Trouble arose again, but not from citizens whose economic interests were threatened by Paul, as had happened in Philippi. Instead, it sprang from the jealousy of the Jews at Paul's success with the Gentiles, particularly the God-fearers who attended synagogues. Paul and Silas had to move to the neighboring town of Berea, where they worked until Jews from Thessalonica incited the Bereans against them. Once more Paul had to leave a new church; he made his way to Athens.

Paul's ministry in Athens illustrates the kind of approach the apostle made to the highly educated. Some Athenians held to a superstitious idolatry, while others embraced a more enlightened philosophy. Paul's words had great relevancy to Epicureans, who thought it unnecessary to seek after God and had no fear of His judgment. His approach also attracted Stoics, who had a pantheistic concept of God. Paul wisely used the insights of these philosophies in his witnessing. For example, Epicureans ridiculed the superstitious, irrational belief in gods as expressed in idolatry; Stoics stressed the unity of humanity and its kinship with God along with the resulting moral duty of individuals. Using the language of Greek philosophy, the apostle was trying to build bridges of thought to reach the Athenian intellectuals. At the same time he thoroughly rooted his speech in Old Testament thought and in the gospel. He focused on God as Creator and on how to worship Him properly.

Paul began his speech with an introduction designed to attract his audience's attention and to state his theme—the ignorance of pagan worship. The main body of the address fell into three parts: (1) God is Lord of the whole world; He needs no temple or human worship rituals. (2) People are God's creation; they need God. (3) Being made by God, people cannot make God into an idol. Paul called on his audience to abandon their ignorant ideas of God and to repent, for God has set a day of judgment by Him who was raised from the dead.

THE LESSON PASSAGE

1. Paul's Witness to the Thessalonians (Acts 17:1-4)

After leaving Philippi, Paul and his missionary companions traveled through Amphipolis and Apollonia to Thessalonica. Thessalonica, the capital city of Macedonia, was the largest city of that province. With the finest harbor of the province and its location on the Via Egnatia, the city had great commercial importance. Thessalonica was a free city, having its own assembly and self-rule. Among its large population were Jews who had been drawn to the city by its economic advantages.

In the synagogue for three Sabbaths Paul reasoned from the Scriptures, using them to show that the Messiah would suffer and rise from the dead. He argued that these prophecies had their fulfillment in Jesus. Paul's preaching in the Thessalonian synagogue had encouraging results. Some Jews believed and joined Paul and Silas. The greatest response came from the God-fearing Gentiles, including a few prominent women.

2. The Jews' Opposition to Paul (Acts 17:5-9)

When the Jews saw many of the God-fearing Gentiles following the teachings of Paul and Silas, they became jealous and angry. Such Gentiles represented the best prospects for conversion to Judaism. So the Jews recruited a mob to go after the missionaries. The mob looked for Paul and Silas at the home of Jason, likely one of the Jewish converts who had offered hospitality to the missionaries.

Not finding the missionaries, the crowd dragged Jason and other believers before the city authorities. This rabble made two accusations against Paul and his coworker. First, they contended that these men were causing trouble all over the Roman Empire. Second and more seriously, they declared that Paul and Silas had acted contrary to the decrees of the emperor by stating there was another king, Jesus.

The city authorities took such charges seriously, fearing Rome would censure them for harboring state enemies. The officials made Jason and the other believers "post bond" (17:9) and then released them. Jason had to guarantee the good behavior of his friends. This led to Paul and Silas's leaving the city. Paul's Letters to the Thessalonians indicate that the believers of Thessalonica were severely persecuted after Paul's departure.

3. Paul's Witness to the Bereans (Acts 17:10-12)

The believers sent Paul and Silas away to Berea, about 50 miles south and west of Thessalonica. Evidently Timothy joined them there. In Berea the missionaries again went first to the synagogue. Paul proclaimed the messianic hope set forth in the Old Testament and its fulfillment in Jesus. The Berean hearers welcomed his message with great eagerness and examined the Scriptures to determine whether or not these things were so. As a result, many of the Jews believed, as did also a number of prominent Greek women and many Greek men.

4. Paul's Flight to Athens (Acts 17:13-15)

When news of Paul's preaching and the gospel's success in Berea reached the Jewish community in Thessalonica, a number of the Thessalonian Jews came to Berea to disrupt the work. Again Paul was forced to leave a city where the Christian faith had been planted with great promise. The new believers quickly escorted Paul to the coast and on to Athens, probably by sea, while Silas and Timothy remained in Macedonia. Paul wanted his associates to join him as soon as possible.

Situated in the Roman province of Achaia, Athens had reigned as the most noted city of ancient Greece. The city had reached its golden age in the fourth and fifth centuries B.C. Athens attracted intellectuals from all over the world. Politically it became a democracy. Such figures as Socrates, Plato, Aristotle, Epicurus, and Zeno lived there. Philip II of Macedon conquered Athens in 338 B.C. This resulted in the spread of Athenian culture and learning into Asia and Egypt through his son, Alexander the Great. The Romans conquered Athens in 146 B.C. Under their rule Athens continued as the cultural and intellectual center of the Roman Empire. Rome also left the city politically free. By the time Paul came to Athens, it had long since lost its empire and wealth. Corinth had become the leading city of Greece commercially and politically at this time. Athens was in a period of decline, tending to live on its reputation.

5. Paul's Witness to the Athenians (Acts 17:16-34)

Verse 16: *While Paul was waiting for them in Athens, he was greatly distressed to see that the city was full of idols.*

While Paul was waiting for Silas and Timothy, he got acquainted with **Athens.** As an educated man, Paul already knew the reputation of the city with its magnificent art and architecture. He found himself personally confronted with its pagan and idolatrous culture. He saw art depicting the activities of the various Greek gods and goddesses. The most famous buildings were actually temples to pagan gods. Paul found the scene repulsive. The Greek behind *greatly distressed* is strong. It describes Paul as being angry and irritated at the overwhelming evidence of idolatry.

The sight of a city so entirely dedicated to false worship moved Paul to action. Following his usual pattern, he reasoned with the Jews and God-fearing Gentiles in the synagogue on the Sabbath. During the week he witnessed to all who would listen in the agora, the marketplace and center of Athenian life. When a group of Epicurean and Stoic philosophers heard Paul speaking in the marketplace, they began to argue with him.

Athens was the home of the rival Epicurean and Stoic schools of philosophy. Epicureans believed pleasure was the chief goal of life, especially mental pleasures such as tranquility. The ideal life for Epicureans was one free from pain, disturbing passions, superstitious fears, and anxiety about death. They did not deny the existence of gods but argued that deities took no interest in people's lives. The Stoics emphasized reason and individual self-sufficiency. They were basically pantheists, believing there was a divine, rational, ordering principle in all things and beings. Their goal centered on living harmoniously with nature. The Stoics generally held high principles related to ethical and civic duties.

These Athenian philosophers had two comments about Paul (17:18). First, they labeled him a "babbler." This negative word pictured a bird picking up and dropping seeds. It came to mean those who snapped up ideas of others and peddled them as their own without understanding them. Second, they said Paul seemed to advocate "foreign gods." When Paul spoke of Jesus and the resurrection, they likely thought he was referring to a male god and his female consort or goddess, *Anastasia,* the Greek word for resurrection. The idea of the dead rising was unusual to the Greeks. The Epicureans did not believe in any existence after death; the Stoics believed that only the soul, the divine spark, survived death. Thus they probably thought Paul was using a name, not referring to an event.

The philosophers brought Paul to a meeting of the Areopagus so he could explain his new teaching more fully. "Areopagus" (17:19) could refer either to a location, a council, or to both. The term *Areopagus* means hill of Ares. Ares was the Greek god of war. The same Roman god was called Mars, hence the translation in some Bibles, "Mars Hill." Bible students have debated whether Luke meant to describe a meeting of the court to try Paul's teaching (whether formally or informally) or an unofficial gathering of Athenians on the Areopagus to hear him lecture. Luke characterized the Athenians as having a great curiosity for the latest ideas (17:21). Their curiosity enabled Paul to witness.

Verse 22: *Paul then stood up in the meeting of the Areopagus and said: "Men of Athens! I see that in every way you are very religious.*

Paul began his address by noting that he was impressed with the ***very religious*** nature of the Athenians. *Religious* could be used in a positive sense for those devoted to religious matters. So the apostle could have been commending the Athenians to gain the favorable attention of the audience. However, the word also had a negative meaning; it was used of those who were overly scrupulous, even superstitious, in their religious observances. Perhaps Paul deliberately chose an ambiguous word. The Athenians might have assumed his remark commended their piety, but Paul could have been thinking of their idolatry.

Verse 23: *For as I walked around and looked carefully at your objects of worship, I even found an altar with this inscription: TO AN UNKNOWN GOD. Now what you worship as something unknown I am going to proclaim to you.*

Paul did not begin his address by referring to Jewish history or by quoting the Scriptures. He knew these Gentile philosophers had no interest in prophecies they had neither read nor accepted as authoritative. Instead, he took for his point of contact ***an altar*** he had seen in the city with the ***inscription: TO AN UNKNOWN GOD.*** Archaeological discoveries have provided evidence of such altars in Athens. The Athenians had erected such an altar because they feared offending some deity of whom they were unaware and had failed to give the proper worship.

Paul did not imply that his hearers were unconscious worshipers of the true God. Rather, he was drawing their attention to Him who was ultimately responsible for all that they attributed to this *UNKNOWN GOD* and all other gods as well. To worship an unknown god is to admit one's ignorance. Paul emphasized their ignorance. They did not know or worship God. They worshiped a ***what***—an object or a thing, not a personal God at all. For Greeks, ignorance was a primary sin. Now Paul was going to ***proclaim*** the truth to them to remove their ignorance.

Verse 24: *"The God who made the world and everything in it is the Lord of heaven and earth and does not live in temples built by hands.*

Paul proclaimed ***the God*** of biblical revelation ***who made the world*** and all that it contains and who is, therefore, *the Lord of heaven and earth.* Many Greeks would have had difficulty accepting the concept of God as absolute Creator, for they believed one found divinity in the heavens, in nature, and even in humanity. Paul presented the Athenians with a new idea: a single Supreme Being who stood over the world and created *everything* that exists. This opposed all the pantheistic and polytheistic notions of the Athenians.

The God who is Creator and Lord clearly *does not live in temples built by hands.* Paul's words echoed Solomon's prayer at the dedication of the temple when he recognized its inadequacy as a house for God (1 Kings 8:27) as well as Stephen's critique of the temple (Acts 7:48-50). Some Athenian philosophers would have accepted this aspect of God's nature.

Verse 25: *And he is not served by human hands, as if he needed anything, because he himself gives all men life and breath and everything else.*

Paul declared that God is *not served by human hands, as if he needed anything.* He does not depend on people for their worship and service. God needs nothing from His creatures (see Ps. 50:9-12). Far from their supplying any need of His, He is the source of their *life and breath and everything else.* He supplies every need they have. Greek philosophy also viewed divinity as complete within itself, totally self-sufficient and without need. Yet the philosophers' pantheism differed greatly from Paul's monotheism. Paul rooted his teachings in the Old Testament (see Isa. 42:5). The Creator God stands above His creation. He is not a divine principle that pervades all nature and humankind. Although Paul used terms the Athenians understood, he did not compromise biblical truth.

Verse 26: *From one man he made every nation of men, that they should inhabit the whole earth; and he determined the times set for them and the exact places where they should live.*

The One who created all things in general created humanity in particular. The Athenians boasted that they had originated from the soil of their homeland. They believed the Greeks were innately superior to non-Greeks, whom they called barbarians. Contrary to these thoughts, Paul affirmed the oneness of humanity in their creation by the one God and their descent from a common ancestor, *from one man,* Adam. Paul was not proclaiming a local Jewish God but the sovereign Lord of all people.

Having made the entire human race, God also gave them the *whole earth* to dwell in. Part of the forming and furnishing of this dwelling place consisted in the *times set for them and the exact places where they should live. Times* could refer either to the seasons or to historical epochs. *Places* could mean the habitable areas of the planet or the boundaries between nations. Seasons and habitable zones point to God's providence in nature. Historical epochs and national boundaries emphasize God's lordship over history. All of these possible meanings point to God's care for and control over His creation. .

Verse 27: *God did this so that men would seek him and perhaps reach out for him and find him, though he is not far from each one of us.*

God had a purpose for His creation—that people **would seek him.** Seek could have the Greek pagan sense of seeking after and examining what is true. The Stoics believed that through the proper discipline of reason people could come to a knowledge of divinity. The best meaning for Paul's use of *seek* comes from the Old Testament: the thankful and reverent longing of the whole person for the God whose goodness an individual has experienced. It refers mainly to a response of the will—trusting and obeying God—not to an act of the intellect.

Paul used a grammatical form for the next two verbs that expresses strong doubt about the result of seeking: ***perhaps*** people would ***reach out for him and find him.*** *Reach out* refers to the groping of a person in darkness. Despite His transcendence and greatness, the living God *is **not far** from each one of us.* Ironically, however, human beings stumble around trying to find Him. Paul knew people could not find God apart from divine revelation. Self-directed searching for God was made in ignorance.

Verse 28: *'For in him we live and move and have our being.' As some of your own poets have said, 'We are his offspring.'*

To establish common ground with his hearers and to support the Jewish-Christian doctrine of God, Paul quoted Greek poets whom the audience recognized as authorities. Many scholars attribute the statement ***For in him we live and move and have our being*** to the Cretan poet Epimenides (600 B.C.). Paul did not use these words in the Greek sense that stressed the pantheistic view of divinity residing in human nature. He affirmed God as the source of life and energy. The second quote is from the Stoic poet, Aratus (315-240 B.C.), who may have been quoting a hymn to Zeus by the poet Cleanthes. Paul used the words in reference to God. ***We are his offspring*** indicates God created people in His image.

Verse 29: *"Therefore since we are God's offspring, we should not think that the divine being is like gold or silver or stone—an image made by man's design and skill.*

Based on the fact that humans are God's offspring, Paul attacked idolatry. If women and men are made in God's image, then small images of ***gold*** and ***silver,*** massive temple idols of ***stone,*** or any other material figures cannot represent God. An inanimate ***image made by*** human ***design and skill*** cannot portray the living God. Paul echoed the ongoing Jewish argument against idol worship (see Isa. 44:9). Even if Greek philosophers rationalized idols as mere symbols of the unseen divinity, most pagans worshiped the images themselves. Only the worship of God in spirit and in truth is acceptable, not exalting things people have made.

Verse 30: *In the past God overlooked such ignorance, but now he commands all people everywhere to repent.*

The Athenians had worshiped in vain, for they had been ignorant of the one true God. God in mercy, however, had **overlooked such ignorance** (see 2 Pet. 3:9). The proclamation of the gospel brings ends ignorance about God because Christ's coming and work revealed God's true nature. He was no longer unknown to the Athenians. God commanded them **to repent,** to turn completely from their false worship and turn to God.

Verse 31: *For he has set a day when he will judge the world with justice by the man he has appointed. He has given proof of this to all men by raising him from the dead."*

Paul reached the climax of his message. He urgently emphasized the need for repentance by declaring God has appointed a **day** for the judgment of the **world.** This day of judging is **set.** It will be a righteous judgment **(with justice).** All persons must ultimately stand before God and give an account of their lives, including their relationship to Him. Greek thought did not include such a future judgment.

Also God **has appointed** His agent to carry out this judgment. This **man** is Christ in His role as Judge. God **has given proof** of this truth by the miracle of **raising him from the dead.** With these words Paul returned to the theme of his earlier preaching, Jesus and the resurrection. He treated the resurrection as historical fact and used it as proof of the divine appointment of Jesus as Judge.

Verse 32: *When they heard about the resurrection of the dead, some of them sneered, but others said, "We want to hear you again on this subject."*

Paul's return to his starting point, the **resurrection,** provoked the scorn of some of his hearers. The **resurrection** of Jesus from the dead represented only foolishness to the majority of Athenians (1 Cor. 1:23). The Epicureans believed in no human existence after death. The Stoics believed that only the soul survived death. The idea of a bodily, physical resurrection made no sense to the Greeks, not even that of a transformed body. So, many in the Areopagus simply **sneered** at Paul's reference to the resurrection. Others, however, wanted to **hear** him **again on this subject.** Paul had not convinced them, but they were willing to give him an opportunity to explain his views.

Verse 33: *At that, Paul left the Council.*

Those who sneered must have been in the majority because Paul did not remain before the Areopagus. He left the **Council.**

Verse 34: *A few men became followers of Paul and believed. Among them was Dionysius, a member of the Areopagus, also a woman named Damaris, and a number of others.*

A **few** people responded in faith to Paul's witness about the risen Lord: **Dionysius, a member of the Areopagus, also a woman named Damaris,** *and a number of others.* The conversion of *Dionysius* indicates that Paul's audience contained members of the court of the *Areopagus.* We know nothing certain about Dionysius and *Damaris.* The conversions of Damaris and *others* might have resulted from Paul's earlier witness in the synagogue and agora of Athens.

Luke did not present Paul's sermon as a failure, although some commentators view it that way. They point out that the New Testament gives no record of a church at Athens. Also, when Paul spoke of the first converts in Achaia, he referred to the household of Stephanas at Corinth, where he worked after Athens (1 Cor. 16:15). (The assumption that Stephanas's household was converted in Corinth, however, is destroyed by Paul's comment that they were the first saved in Achaia. Obviously, they were converted in Athens during Paul's visit there.) Some have concluded that Paul failed at Athens because he changed his preaching, speaking about providence, being in God, creation, and resurrection, instead of grace, being in Christ, redemption, and the cross. They also fault him for appealing to Greek poets. Yet there were converts at Athens. The number of converts does not minimize the working of God's Spirit. The reason the gospel did not take root lay more in the attitude of the Athenians than in Paul's approach or in what he said.

We have much to learn from Paul's witness in Athens. The apostle attempted to build bridges to the Athenians to win some. He used their language, quoted their poets, seeking to reach them in terms they would understand. Yet Paul never compromised the gospel. His efforts serve as a model for us. We need to learn to witness wisely because we live in a society that has become increasingly pluralistic in its religious beliefs. As wise witnesses we will begin by addressing unbelievers at their levels of spiritual understanding. We will present forthrightly the basic truth of the gospel without compromise. We also will recognize that people will respond in various ways to Christ. Our responsibility rests in witnessing faithfully and leaving the results to God.

FOR FURTHER STUDY

1. Read "Paul and the Thessalonians" in the Winter 1997 issue of the *Biblical Illustrator.*

2. Read "Life After Death in Greco-Roman Religion" in the Spring 1999 issue of *Biblical Illustrator* and "Paul and the Athenians" in the Winter 2000 issue.

3. See "Athens" in the section "Important Cities in Paul's Ministry" in *Holman Bible Atlas,* pages 251-52.

The Week of December 17
PERSISTENT WITNESSING

Background Passage: Acts 18:1-22
Lesson Passage: Acts 18:5-16

INTRODUCTION

Jake first met Sam (names changed) when they worked together in state government. The two became friends and kept up with each other even after Jake left to attend seminary and Sam decided to enter the business world. From the beginning of their relationship they often talked about spiritual issues. Sam understood many facts about the Christian faith and attended church regularly. He knew, however, he was not a Christian. Through the years Jake continued to challenge him to accept Christ as His Savior. Sam feared the Lord would want him to give up his successful business career. After 12 years of patiently witnessing to Sam, Jake received a card from him one day. He had simply written a date, a time, and the words, "I did it." Jake called Sam to rejoice with him in his decision to follow Christ. This new believer related how he had been sitting in an Easter service when he realized that Christ had died for him. He surrendered to the Lord who loved him that much. Jake's wise, loving, and persistent witness resulted in his seeing the Lord work in Sam's life.

This lesson focuses on the apostle Paul's work in Corinth among Jews and Gentiles. It emphasizes his persistence in a witnessing ministry despite rejection and active opposition. We too need to trust and follow God's leadership to witness regularly even though some will not respond.

Acts 18:1-22

1. Paul Met Aquila and Priscilla in Corinth (18:1-3)
2. Paul Witnessed in the Synagogue (18:4-5)
3. Paul Turned to the Gentiles (18:6-8)
4. God Reassured Paul (18:9-11)
5. Gallio Threw Out Paul's Accusers (18:12-17)
6. Paul Traveled to Ephesus and Antioch (18:18-22)

THE BACKGROUND

Corinth lay 50 miles west of Athens and was located on the southern end of a narrow isthmus that connected the Peloponnesus (a peninsula forming the southern part of Greece) with the Greek mainland. Corinth was founded in ancient times and had become the wealthiest Grecian city by 750 B.C. In 146 B.C. the Roman general Mummius, in a fierce act of revenge on the city for an anti-Roman revolt, destroyed Corinth so completely that the site lay abandoned for 100 years. In 46 B.C. Julius Caesar rebuilt Corinth and colonized it with veterans and freedmen. This made it the most Roman city of Greece. The new Corinth soon became the capital of the province of Achaia and regained its prominence .

The city had two ports: Lechaeum on the west gave access to the Adriatic Sea and Cenchrea on the east opened into the Aegean Sea. By including these two seaports, Corinth's population numbered as much as 600,000, making it the largest city of Greece in Paul's day.

Corinth had a favorable position for commerce: it stood at the junction of sea routes to the west and east and land routes to the north and south. This caused the city to prosper greatly. With its economic revival Corinth also experienced a rebirth of its old immoral ways. As early as the fifth century B.C. a Greek verb translated "to live like a Corinthian" meant to live immorally. "Corinthian girl" meant prostitute.

Gross immorality characterized even the religion of Corinth. At the temple of Aphrodite, the Greek goddess of love, located on top of a hill overlooking the city, a thousand young women served as priestesses, actually as religious prostitutes. The city also had temples to other gods, including the sun god, Apollo, the patron god of Corinth, and Asklepius, the Greek god of healing. The presence of a Jewish settlement in Corinth, however, meant the worship of the true God also existed in the city.

Paul spent a year and a half in this key population center during the time of founding the Corinthian church. His letters to the Corinthian believers show his affection for them, but no other church gave him as much trouble and grief as did this congregation. Problems included internal conflicts and the development of unbalanced ideas. These things proved more dangerous to the spiritual growth of the believers than persecution from outside the community of faith.

THE LESSON PASSAGE

1. Paul Met Aquila and Priscilla in Corinth (Acts 18:1-3)

Paul recognized Corinth as an important center for evangelistic work. He thus settled there for a considerable time to establish churches that would evangelize the surrounding areas and witness to the constant stream of sailors and travelers.

As Paul entered this large and thriving city, he might have sought work from a master tentmaker to support himself. Jewish law required rabbis to perform their religious and legal functions without demanding a fee. Consequently, they needed to have some other source of income. Paul earned his living as a tentmaker on his missionary journeys. Some translations render the word *tentmaker* by a more general term, leather worker. Tents often were made of leather. Tentmakers probably used their skills on other types of leather products. Some Bible students have suggested that Paul worked in cilicium, a cloth of woven goat's hair that often was used as a material for tents. Cilicium originated in and derived its name from Paul's native province of Cilicia.

Paul's job search led him to meet the Jewish Christian couple, Priscilla and Aquila, who also worked as tentmakers. Paul joined this husband and wife, living and working with them. The apostle quickly formed a deep and lifelong friendship with this couple. He identified them as his fellow workers and mentioned them in his letters (Rom. 16:3; 1 Cor. 16:19; 2 Tim. 4:19). Paul and Luke always named the two together, never separately. They were a ministry team. Paul referred to the wife as "Prisca," her formal name, while Luke used "Priscilla," a diminutive, familiar designation. Luke often used the less formal form of a name. Aquila, a Latin name, comes from the word for eagle. Priscilla's name often precedes her husband's. That Luke and Paul would name her first was remarkable for the first century. Some suggest Priscilla came from a higher social class than her husband or possessed Roman citizenship. Others think she had more importance in Christian circles. Aquila was a native of Pontus, a region in northern Asia Minor on the southern shore of the Black Sea.

Priscilla and Aquila had recently come to Corinth from Rome because the emperor Claudius had expelled the Jews from the city with an edict issued in A.D. 49. This important detail helps to give a date for Paul's arrival in Corinth and to establish his chronology. Commentators usually connect the emperor's edict with a statement by Suetonius, the second-century A.D. Roman historian. Suetonius noted the Jews in Rome were involved in constant riots because of a "Chrestus," probably a misspelling of "Christ." The dispute in the Jewish community was between those who accepted Jesus Christ as Messiah and those who rejected Him.

Christianity probably came to Rome quite early as a result of the constant flow of travelers to and from the capital city. The Roman government would have identified Jewish Christians as ringleaders in the unrest over Chrestus. Consequently, believers were forced to leave the capital, including Priscilla and Aquila. They already were Christians before they met with Paul; otherwise, Luke surely would have told of their conversion.

2. Paul Witnessed in the Synagogue (Acts 18:4-5)

While working with Priscilla and Aquila, Paul followed his usual custom of attending the local synagogue every Sabbath. There he reasoned with those present, trying to persuade both Jews and God-fearing Gentiles that Jesus is the Christ. The apostle may have wanted to refrain from a more active ministry in Corinth until Silas and Timothy could join him.

Verse 5: *When Silas and Timothy came from Macedonia, Paul devoted himself exclusively to preaching, testifying to the Jews that Jesus was the Christ.*

The arrival of Silas and Timothy in Corinth changed Paul's situation. They brought good news about the Christians at Thessalonica and perhaps a gift of money from the congregation at Philippi (2 Cor. 11:9). The news from Thessalonica concerning the believers' spiritual well-being greatly comforted and encouraged Paul. Money from the Macedonian Christians and/or the work of Silas and Timothy supplied his needs, giving him freedom from having to earn a living. The apostle did not impose any burden on the Corinthian believers by asking financial support from them (1 Cor. 9:12). He certainly did not want the Corinthians to identify him with the dishonest traveling teachers who made a profit from peddling their message, such as some Cynic philosophers.

Paul was able to devote himself *exclusively to preaching* throughout the week, not just on the Sabbath. He proclaimed *to the Jews that Jesus was the Christ,* the Messiah foretold in the Old Testament. During this time, Paul probably wrote 1 Thessalonians in response to the report Silas and Timothy had brought from Thessalonica. Some while later, on learning of continued confusion at Thessalonica regarding the return of Christ and the believers' relation to it, he wrote 2 Thessalonians.

3. Paul Turned to the Gentiles (Acts 18:6-8)

Verse 6: *But when the Jews opposed Paul and became abusive, he shook out his clothes in protest and said to them, "Your blood be on your own heads! I am clear of my responsibility. From now on I will go to the Gentiles."*

Paul's ministry at Corinth followed the pattern set at Pisidian Antioch on the first missionary journey. After his initial preaching in the synagogue, the majority of Jews *opposed Paul and became abusive.* The apostle had done his best to convince them of the seriousness of their condition in rejecting the gospel. Now he turned directly *to the Gentiles.* In solemn Old Testament style *Paul shook out his clothes in protest* (see Neh. 5:13). This act symbolized several things. It showed that Paul had broken fellowship with the Jews. It protested the Jews' opposition and cleared the apostle from further *responsibility* for them. It also showed his displeasure against what he considered the Jews' blasphemy. Jews often performed this action—shaking out their clothes—against Gentiles. Paul's act showed that those Jews who rejected the gospel were no better than the Gentiles. They cut themselves off from the true people of God.

If the Jews found themselves ultimately rejected by God, the responsibility would rest entirely with themselves. Paul had preached faithfully to them. He had no blame for how they responded. From this point forward in Corinth, he focused his efforts on the Gentiles, including Jewish proselytes and others.

Verse 7: *Then Paul left the synagogue and went next door to the house of Titius Justus, a worshiper of God.*

When Paul **left the synagogue,** he moved his place of witness **next door to the house of Titius Justus.** As a **worshiper of God** this man was a God-fearing Gentile who had attended services and received instruction at the synagogue. He must have believed Paul's message since he invited the missionary to make his home the headquarters for the work in Corinth. The *house of Titius Justus,* therefore, became the first meeting place of the Corinthian church. People used to attending the synagogue did not have to travel far if they wished to continue hearing Paul. This location for Paul's preaching probably did not make for good relations with the Jews, but it was perfect for influencing those who went to the synagogue. This bold move also reflected Paul's desire to continue to try to convert Jews, even though he would be outside the synagogue and focusing his efforts on Gentiles.

Some Bible students identify *Titius Justus* with Gaius. Romans customarily had three names, so these students assume that *Titius* and *Justus* are the last two names, the first name being Gaius. Paul wrote of Gaius, "whose hospitality I and the whole church here [at Corinth] enjoy" (Rom. 16:23). Also Paul spoke of a Gaius he personally baptized at the beginning of his ministry in Corinth (1 Cor. 1:14). Presumably he was referring to this man who hosted the Christian mission when it needed a place to meet after being forced to leave the synagogue.

Verse 8: *Crispus, the synagogue ruler, and his entire household believed in the Lord; and many of the Corinthians who heard him believed and were baptized.*

Paul's move to the neighboring property proved fruitful. **Many of the Corinthians** heard the gospel and **believed and were baptized.** The context suggests the converts at this point came from the synagogue—Jews and Gentile God-fearers. Among them was **Crispus,** who served as the **synagogue ruler.** The *synagogue ruler* was a layperson, appointed by the local elders, who cared for the building and selected those who participated in the services. *Crispus* believed in the Lord together with **his entire household.** Paul himself baptized this man (1 Cor. 1:14). The conversion of this leader must have made a strong impression and led to other conversions. It probably also angered the Jews. The commitment to Christ of a synagogue ruler probably led to a crisis among the Jews that resulted in the accusation against Paul they made to Gallio (18:12).

We would do well to follow Paul's example. When a particular individual or group rejects the gospel, we should witness to those who may be more receptive. Paul's persistent witnessing resulted in the conversion of an important leader and many others. Let us witness persistently.

4. God Reassured Paul (Acts 18:9-11)

Verse 9: *One night the Lord spoke to Paul in a vision: "Do not be afraid; keep on speaking, do not be silent.*

Paul had come to Corinth burdened by the problems in Macedonia and his dismissal at Athens. On this missionary trip he had faced strong opposition from both his fellow Jews and some Gentiles in Philippi, Thessalonica, and Berea. The apostle started his ministry in Corinth "in weakness and fear, and with much trembling" (1 Cor. 2:3). He wondered how these Greeks and Roman colonists would receive him.

Already the familiar pattern of strong Jewish opposition had begun. Paul must have asked himself if he would have to leave Corinth under pressure as he had done before in other cities.

One night the Lord graciously gave Paul a *vision* to strengthen him for extensive witness in Corinth. The *vision* led the missionary to decide to remain in Corinth. Its message reflected language used by God Himself in the Old Testament when addressing His servants. This biblical pattern showed God or God's representative confronting and commissioning someone for a task, reassuring that person of help or protection or both (see Ex. 3:2-12; Josh. 1:1-9; Jer. 1:5-10; Isa. 41:10-14). Acts already had included similar incidents (9:10-18; 16:6-10). In Paul's case at Corinth, God recommissioned him. The Greek verbal form of the Lord's command meant that Paul should stop being *afraid.* He was to *keep on speaking, do not be silent.* The apostle should continue his preaching. God addressed Paul's fears about his opponents in Corinth. Instead of fearing what they might do to him, Paul was to proclaim the gospel fearlessly.

Verse 10: *For I am with you, and no one is going to attack and harm you, because I have many people in this city."*

The Lord backed up His command with a promise, *"I am with you."* This assurance of the Lord's presence also gave Paul confidence that he could fulfill the Lord's command. As a result of divine protection, no one in Corinth would be able to *attack and harm* the apostle. The Lord did not say that no one would lay hands on Paul, only that no one would harm him.

Furthermore, the Lord declared that He had *many people in this city.* This seems to mean many in Corinth would be converted, Gentiles as well as Jews. A great work remained for Paul in Corinth. Hostility would not prevent him from continuing that work until God had completed His purposes. At this critical point in Paul's life God gave him a vision to strengthen him for what lay ahead and to guide him. God would keep him safe, and he would see fruit from his evangelistic work.

Verse 11: *So Paul stayed for a year and a half, teaching them the word of God.*

With such a promising start and encouraged by the vision, Paul continued to minister at Corinth for 18 months. During those 18 months, Paul taught the Corinthians the **word of God.** Many people believed and joined the fellowship.

The Lord also has given us the assurance of His presence (Matt. 28:19-20). Thus we may witness persistently without fear or hesitation.

5. Gallio Threw Out Paul's Accusers (Acts 18:12-17)

Verse 12: *While Gallio was proconsul of Achaia, the Jews made a united attack on Paul and brought him into court.*

Paul had received a divine promise that no harm would come to him through any attack in Corinth, but he was not promised freedom from difficulties. As more and more people responded to Paul's preaching, his Jewish opponents *made a united attack* on him and laid a charge against him.

The Jews' method of opposition this time had potentially serious consequences. Instead of stirring up the city rabble against the apostle or accusing him before the civil magistrates, these opponents approached the Roman administration of the province. Evidently the Jews seized the opportunity afforded by the arrival of the new *proconsul of Achaia* to make this attack on Paul. The apostle probably had been preaching in Corinth for eight or nine months before *Gallio* came to this position. The verdict of a Roman proconsul would not only take effect within his province, but officials of other provinces would follow his decision. The appearance of Paul before Gallio had importance because it established a precedent for the manner in which Roman leaders would consider charges against Christians. Had the proconsul of Achaia pronounced a verdict unfavorable to Paul, the story of the progress of Christianity during the next decade or so might have been different.

Both ancient literary sources, such as Seneca and Tacitus, and inscriptions relate details about *Gallio.* He was the son of a Spanish orator. When he came to Rome, a Roman family adopted him. His brother was the famous Stoic philosopher, Seneca. Gallio had a reputation for personal charm but suffered from ill-health. He died as a result of Nero's suspicions against his family. His service in Corinth occurred during the proconsular period of his career. At this time Achaia was a province of second rank, administered by proconsuls. The title *proconsul* showed

Luke's accuracy in writing, for the status of provinces changed with the times. Proconsuls in this region usually served a one-year term, two at the most, beginning in the early summer. An inscription discovered at Delphi, relating to the dedication of an aqueduct, mentions Gallio. This enables scholars to date his proconsulship beginning around July, A.D. 51. This provides an important reference point for determining the date of Paul's work in Corinth as well as for establishing the entire Pauline chronology. Putting Gallio's time in office (18:12) together with Claudius's edict, Paul's 18 months in Corinth could have occurred roughly between early A.D. 50 and late A.D. 52.

The Jews **brought** Paul **into court.** The *court* (Greek, *bema*) was a raised platform that stood in the marketplace in front of the proconsul's residence. It served as a forum or place of public assembly where he tried cases. We do not know whether the Jews dragged Paul forcibly before the governor or whether the apostle appeared of his own free will to answer the charge against him.

Verse 13: *"This man," they charged, "is persuading the people to worship God in ways contrary to the law."*

Did these opponents refer to Jewish or Roman *law?* Why would they expect the Roman proconsul to enforce their own religious *law?* Perhaps the Jews deliberately made the charge ambiguous, hoping Gallio would think Paul acted against Roman religion. There were Roman laws against foreign cults proselytizing Roman citizens, but Gallio obviously did not see the situation in this sense. Judaism was a legitimate, official religion in the eyes of Rome. Paul's Jewish opponents refused to recognize the gospel that he preached as having anything to do with their Jewish faith. They completely rejected Christianity and contended it had no right to claim the protection afforded to adherents of Judaism. Therefore, they argued, the government should stop Paul's preaching and punish him for his activity in spreading his ideas. The Jews might have been appealing also to an edict of the emperor Claudius guaranteeing them freedom of worship and protection from official harassment. They could have claimed that Paul was interfering with their privilege to worship according to their own ways.

Verse 14: *Just as Paul was about to speak, Gallio said to the Jews, "If you Jews were making a complaint about some misdemeanor or serious crime, it would be reasonable for me to listen to you.*

Although **Paul** was ready to defend himself against his opponents' accusations, Gallio cut him off. The proconsul did not see the charge as deserving his time as an official. He would have acted on the complaint had it dealt with criminal behavior, *some misdemeanor or serious crime.* In that area the governor had considerable freedom to dispense justice according to local custom and his own wisdom. *Gallio* believed Paul's alleged conduct did not fall into the class of crime against the state.

Verse 15: *But since it involves questions about words and names and your own law—settle the matter yourselves. I will not be a judge of such things."*

Gallio viewed the whole affair as an internal quarrel in the Jewish community. He saw it as a religious debate about *words and names* and their *own law. Words* could refer to the Scriptures or the message of the gospel. *Names* could relate to identifying Jesus as the expected Messiah. *Law* suggests particular interpretations or requirements of the Jewish law. Whatever the Jews' intention, Gallio understood that the *law* about which they had spoken in their accusation to be their own Jewish law. He rightly argued that he had no call as a Roman official to interfere in such a matter. In Gallio's view, Paul was proclaiming simply a variety of Judaism the leaders of the Jewish community in Corinth did not like. He had no intention of judging on such a matter. He declared they must *settle the matter* themselves. Throughout Acts, no government official ever found the apostle guilty of having broken any Roman law.

Verse 16: *So he had them ejected from the court.*

Gallio finally drove the Jews away from the *court* as an indication that he did not wish to listen to their complaints any further. He probably *ejected* Paul along with the Jews.

Had Gallio accepted the Jewish charge and found Paul guilty, provincial governors everywhere would have had a precedent to restrict Paul's ministry. Gallio's refusal to act in the matter in effect gave recognition to Christianity as a legitimate religion. Later, in the 60's, Rome reversed its position toward Judaism and Christianity; but for the next decade believers proclaimed the gospel message in the provinces of the empire without fear of coming into conflict with Roman law.

"They" then attacked Sosthenes, the synagogue ruler, and beat him in front of the court (18:17). Who did the beating? Perhaps the Jews did. Sosthenes may have served jointly with Crispus (before his conversion) in the local synagogue at Corinth. Larger Jewish synagogues sometimes had more than one leader. Or, he could have taken Crispus's place after the latter became a believer. The Jews may have beaten Sosthenes because they thought he was a Christian sympathizer. A "Sosthenes" served as Paul's secretary in writing to the Corinthian believers from Ephesus (1 Cor. 1:1). Possibly Crispus's successor also converted to Christianity. On the other hand, the Gentiles may have been the ones doing the beating. Gallio's ejection of the Jews may have caused an outbreak of the anti-Semitism always near the surface in the Greco-Roman world. The synagogue ruler, who probably was the chief spokesman against Paul, now received himself the punishment he had wished on the apostle. While we cannot be sure who "they" were, Gallio showed no concern whatever. He refused to have anything to do with the matter.

The gospel has withstood opposition for almost two thousand years. This fact can encourage us when we face opposition to witnessing about Christ. The One in us is greater than the one in the world (1 John 4:4).

6. Paul Traveled to Ephesus and Antioch (Acts 18:18-22)

Paul continued his ministry at Corinth with no legal hindrance and with considerable success for some time after Gallio's decision. The apostle decided to leave Corinth, probably because he wanted to go to Jerusalem to complete a vow he had taken at some unspecified time. Some Greek texts assume Paul wanted to be in Jerusalem for one of the feasts, either Passover or Pentecost. At Cenchrea, the port of departure and the Aegean harbor of Corinth, Paul cut his hair in connection with his vow. This appeared to have been a Nazarite vow (Num. 6:1-21). Paul's reasons for making such a vow remain unclear. People making a Nazarite vow fulfilled it at Jerusalem by presenting the hair to God and offering sacrifices. The vow showed that Paul remained a loyal, practicing Jew. In his mission to the Gentiles, he did not abandon his Jewishness nor stop his witnessing in the synagogue.

From Cenchrea Paul, Priscilla, and Aquila sailed to Ephesus, a port of call for ships traveling from Corinth to the Syrian coast. Priscilla and Aquila remained in this city and continued their Christian witnessing after Paul's departure. Paul, having wanted earlier to minister at Ephesus, went into the synagogue and reasoned with the Jews gathered there. Though he found a receptive audience who encouraged him to stay, fulfilling his vow at Jerusalem took priority over everything else. The apostle promised to return, if God willed (18:21). This brief stop set the stage for Paul's third missionary journey.

The apostle sailed on to Caesarea. He went to Jerusalem and greeted the church. After visiting with the believers there, he went to Antioch of Syria, some 300 miles north. There he reported and ministered to the church that originally had commissioned him to reach the Gentiles. Paul's second missionary journey finally had ended.

FOR FURTHER STUDY

1. Read "Corinth's Moral Climate" in the Summer 1997 issue of *Biblical Illustrator.*

2. Read "Corinth's Religious Atmosphere" in the Summer 1997 issue of *Biblical Illustrator.*

3. Read "Priscilla and Aquila: Paul's Fellow Workers" in the Winter 1997 issue of *Biblical Illustrator.*

The Week of December 24

CELEBRATING JESUS' BIRTH

Background Passage: Matthew 1:18—2:12
Lesson Passage: Matthew 2:1-12

INTRODUCTION

The activities of December can often overwhelm us. Many of us have decorations to display, presents to buy, open houses to attend, travel to arrange, relatives to visit, and traffic to endure. Church itself can become a whirl of activities as choirs practice and perform special music, members decorate the auditorium, classes deliver fruit baskets to shut-ins and gather for fellowships. We also have opportunities to attend special Christmas Eve and other Advent services. The way we observe Christmas makes us busier than usual and often creates stress.

How should we celebrate the birth of our Lord Jesus Christ? Some of the things mentioned previously do help us glorify Him in appropriate ways. What motivates us to follow these traditions? Do we reflect on the meaning of our actions, or are we simply repeating what we have done in past years?

This lesson centers on the Magi's worship of Jesus. It shows that they worshiped Him with purpose and joy at great cost and inconvenience to themselves. As we consider their actions, let us plan appropriate ways we ourselves will celebrate the birth of Christ.

Matthew 1:18—2:12
1. Jesus' Miraculous Conception (1:18)
2. God's Word to Joseph (1:19-21)
3. Prophet's Word Fulfilled (1:22-25)
4. Magi's Adoration (2:1-2,9-12)
5. Herod's Hatred (2:3-8)

THE BACKGROUND

Matthew placed a priority on showing how Jesus fulfilled the Old Testament teachings about the Messiah. Through including the visit of the Magi, he made specific references to the fulfillment of Scriptures by Jesus' birth and also alluded to another messianic passage (Num. 24:17). This Gospel writer approached the Christmas story from Joseph's perspective instead of Mary's. He did not focus on Jesus' birth but on events that happened after it. He alone recorded the visit of the Magi to Jesus' family. In this incident Matthew clearly showed the contrast between these seekers and Herod. He presented Jesus as the true King of the Jews as opposed to the unworthy King Herod. The Magi recognized and worshiped the Christ child for who He was even though they came from pagan backgrounds. Herod, however, even though he served as the ruler of Israel and had professed conversion to Judaism, rejected the new-born King and plotted to destroy Him.

Matthew presented Jesus as the Savior of all nations. The story of the Magi's visit shows how the Gentile world received the newborn King. Those from afar worshiped Him; those at home expressed hostility. This foreshadowed how those to whom Paul presented the gospel on his missionary journeys would respond—typically Christ was received by the Gentiles and rejected by the Jews.

THE LESSON PASSAGE

1. Jesus' Miraculous Conception (Matt. 1:18)

Jesus was miraculously conceived of a virgin through the working of the Holy Spirit. Jesus' conception occurred at a time when Mary was "pledged to be married" or betrothed to Joseph. If Mary's family followed typical Jewish custom, she probably was a young teenager. Joseph was likely much older. In Jewish law a betrothal, which lasted about one year, was far more significant than a modern engagement. Ancient Judaism considered a betrothal legally binding. It could end only by death or divorce, just as a full marriage. Society already referred to a betrothed man as a husband, but the woman remained in her father's house. The marriage was formalized when the husband took the woman to his home. The law did not permit sexual relations and living together under one roof until after this public marriage.

Matthew emphasized that Jesus' conception took place "before" Mary and Joseph "came together," meaning before they had been together as husband and wife. The Gospel writer clearly described a supernatural conception through the Holy Spirit. The context presupposes that both Mary and Joseph had been pure. Pagan myths related the coming together of gods and humans in vulgar physical terms. Matthew did not imply this at all in relation to Jesus' conception. Instead, the power of the Lord, manifested in the Holy Spirit, miraculously brought about that conception. Matthew stated that Mary was "found to be with child." This meant that her pregnancy had become obvious, not that she tried to conceal her condition.

2. God's Word to Joseph (Matt. 1:19-21)

Matthew described Mary's husband, Joseph, as "a righteous man." This referred to a person who was law-abiding, upright in character, and generally obedient and faithful to God's commands. Joseph knew nothing of the miraculous conception brought about by the Holy Spirit. He naturally assumed that Mary had broken her vow of faithfulness. Since he was a righteous man, Joseph could not in good conscience finalize his marriage to this woman whom he thought unfaithful. Such a marriage would have implied his own guilt in the matter. Joseph, however, wanted to spare Mary the disgrace of public divorce, censure, and the legal proceedings for a suspected adulterer. In the Old Testament the penalty for unchastity before marriage was death by stoning (Deut. 22:13-21), but Jews rarely carried that out in the first century. By that time divorce was the rule (based on Deut. 24:1). The law also allowed for private divorce before two witnesses. Joseph proposed to divorce Mary "quietly," which meant privately in the sense of a settlement out of court. This would enable him both to conform to the law and to show compassion.

Joseph tried to solve the problem of Mary's pregnancy in what seemed to him the best way possible. God intervened to change his plans. "An angel of the Lord appeared to him in a dream." Dreams represented an important form of divine communication in the Old Testament and in Matthew's Gospel. Also an angel of the Lord frequently conveyed God's instructions to His people. The Greek word *angelos* originally meant messenger. This angelic messenger first reminded Joseph of his messianic lineage by calling him "son of David." The command "do not be afraid to take Mary home" confirmed that Joseph had already decided to divorce Mary when God intervened. Instead, Joseph was "to take Mary home as his wife," an expression reflecting the marriage customs of the day. The angel further explained to Joseph that Mary had not been unfaithful and that her child was not the result of unfaithfulness but had been conceived by the direct action of the Holy Spirit.

The angel told Joseph that Mary would "give birth to a son." When the marriage was formalized, Mary's child would legally become Joseph's and thus a son of David. Gabriel had already told Mary the child's name (Luke 1:31). Now God revealed that same name to Joseph and gave the reason for it. Jesus is the Greek form of Joshua or Jeshua, a common name in those days. It meant Yahweh (the Lord) is salvation or the Lord saves. His name explained the main purpose of Jesus' coming: to "save His people from their sins." His people would be the Jews first, but Matthew anticipated a wider ultimate application (Matt. 28:19). Jesus' ministry would not involve the physical liberation of Israelites from their enemies but their spiritual salvation. He would remove the separation from God that their sins had created. He would accomplish this by giving His own life as a payment for the penalty of their sins.

3. Prophet's Word Fulfilled (Matt. 1:22-25)

Matthew quoted Isaiah 7:14 as being fulfilled in the conception of Jesus. God was working out His purposes in the events the angel had prophesied. Interpreters debate the meaning of the Hebrew word *almah*, the word Isaiah used for "virgin." Some declare that it refers to a young woman of marriageable age. However, the translators of the Septuagint, an ancient translation of the Hebrew Old Testament into Greek, understood the word to mean *virgin*. Also, nowhere in the Old Testament is the word used of a married woman. Apparently Isaiah's original prophecy to Ahaz meant that an unmarried and unidentified virgin would marry and bear a child. Before that child was old enough to know right from wrong, the kings Ahaz dreaded would be destroyed (Isa. 7:15-16). However, that was but a partial fulfillment of Isaiah's God-inspired words.

God inspired Matthew to reveal that the prophecy had a complete and literal fulfillment in the virgin birth of Jesus. A "virgin," Mary, conceived by the power of the Holy Spirit. That conception was unique, unlike any before or after. While Jesus probably never used "Immanuel" as an actual name, the title indicates His incarnate identity—"God with us."

In keeping with his righteous character Joseph obeyed the Lord's commands as given through the angel. He submitted to the Lord and took Mary home as his wife. What he did took great courage. God's message to him had given him confidence in the truth of Mary's virginity. Just as Mary's submission to the Lord came at great cost to her, so did Joseph's. He gave the protection of his spotless reputation and his lineage to Mary and her infant Son. Matthew wanted to make Jesus' virgin conception quite clear, so he added that Joseph had no sexual union with Mary "until she gave birth" to Jesus. Joseph was not Jesus' biological father. Though the couple formally completed their marriage, they did not consummate it before the birth of Jesus.

4. Magi's Adoration (Matt. 2:1-2,9-12)

Verse 1: *After Jesus was born in Bethlehem in Judea, during the time of King Herod, Magi from the east came to Jerusalem*

The Magi's visit to Jesus took place **after** He was **born in Bethlehem in Judea.** How long after the birth the visit occurred is uncertain. Perhaps one to two years had passed, for at that time Joseph and Mary were living in a house (Matt. 2:11). Also Herod gave orders to murder all the boys two and under in Bethlehem (Matt. 2:16). This hardly would have been necessary if the birth had taken place recently. Matthew identified *Bethlehem* as the one *in Judea* to distinguish it from the Bethlehem in Galilee ("Zebulun" in Josh. 19:15). *Bethlehem* means house of bread. Ruth met Boaz in this Bethlehem (Ruth 1:22—2:6). It was the home of David, descendent of Ruth and legally the ancestor of Jesus.

Matthew specified the time of Jesus' birth as *during the time of King Herod. Herod* died in 4 B.C. Jesus was probably born a year or two before that, around 6 or 5 B.C. (The sixth-century monk who developed the Christian calendar did not have accurate information about the time of Herod's death.) Herod the Great was half-Jew, half-Idumean (Edomite). He ascended to power as client-ruler of Israel in 37 B.C. by crushing all opposition to his rule with the help of Roman forces. Herod was wealthy, politically gifted, intensely loyal, and clever enough to remain in the good graces of successive Roman emperors. He also was an excellent administrator. Even his enemies admired his building projects, including the temple in Jerusalem. Yet Herod loved power, inflicted heavy taxes on the people, and conscripted labor from the Israelites. He resented that many Jews considered him a usurper. In his last years he suffered from an illness that increased his paranoia about threats against his person and throne. In fits of rage and jealously he killed close associates, his wife Mariamne, and at least two of his sons.

Several centuries earlier, *Magi* referred to a priestly caste of Medes who claimed special power to interpret dreams. In later centuries down to New Testament times, the word generally covered a wide variety of those interested in dreams, astrology, and magic. Some *Magi* honestly did seek after truth; many were dishonest cheats. Some scholars believe these figures held both political and religious roles and had some prominence in their own country. These *Magi* came to Jerusalem *from the east,* either Arabia, Babylon, Persia, or elsewhere. Matthew did not name the *Magi* or tell how many there were. By the end of the sixth century, writers had given them names: Melkon (later Melchior), Balthasar, and Gasper. The idea of the Magi being three men is based on the number of gifts given the Christ child (Matt. 2:11).

Verse 2: *and asked, "Where is the one who has been born king of the Jews? We saw his star in the east and have come to worship him."*

The Magi's question to Herod about the *king of the Jews* emphasized the word *born.* They specifically asked about the child who had legitimate claim to Israel's throne by virtue of His birth. Jesus' kingly status belonged to Him from birth. Matthew had already established Jesus' participation in the Davidic dynasty by the genealogy (1:1-17). The Magi's question made Herod truly seem to be a usurper to the throne. Jesus was indeed the true King in contrast to Herod. The rule of Jesus as King, however, had a different sense from what that title conveyed to the Roman ruler, his soldiers, and the Jewish leaders.

The Magi had come to Jerusalem because they had seen the King's *star in the east. In the east* could mean that they were in the East when they saw the star. More than likely, however, it means the Magi saw the star at its rising or when it arose. This new heavenly feature had attracted their attention. Several ancient accounts, both pagan and Jewish, told of stars heralding the birth of great persons. So the Magi's question rose naturally from their observation. Matthew may have recalled Balaam's prophecy of the rising of a star out of Jacob (Num. 24:17). The Jews understood this to refer to the coming Deliverer, the Messiah.

The Magi did not tell how their astrology led them to seek a King of the Jews or what made them think that this particular star was His. The Magi might have linked the star to the King of the Jews through studying the Old Testament and other Jewish writings. Nor did the Magi explain the exact nature of the star. Scholars have suggested various possibilities of a regular astronomical phenomenon to identify the star: a coming together of planets in the sky, a comet, or a nova (a star that appears temporarily with great brightness due to an explosion). None of these satisfactorily account for the timing and behavior of the star that led the Magi (see 2:9-10). It seems to have been a sign by God for a specific purpose.

The Magi came to *worship* this newborn King. *Worship* does not necessarily imply that the Magi recognized Jesus' divinity. It may simply mean to do homage or pay respect to a person of high rank. Matthew, however, frequently used *worship* in contexts where others recognized Jesus' more-than-human status. He might have implied that meaning here as well, especially since he already had told of the virgin conception.

The Old Testament mocks astrologers and forbids astrology. Matthew did not condemn or approve this activity. Instead, he contrasted the eagerness of the Magi to worship Jesus to the disinterest of the Jewish leaders and the hostility of Herod.

Verse 9: *After they had heard the king, they went on their way, and the star they had seen in the east went ahead of them until it stopped over the place where the child was.*

The Magi went first to Jerusalem because they assumed the ruler of the Jews would naturally be born in the capital city. Now **after they had heard [through] the king** about Bethlehem as the birthplace, **they went on their way. Went ahead** could mean that the star led them on without itself moving, but the words **stopped over** means literally *came and stood.* This indicates the star itself moved to guide the Magi to Bethlehem. The text does not say whether or not the star had moved in this way previously. The **place where the child was** may or may not have indicated the precise house. It could have meant that the star simply hovered over the town of Bethlehem, the general location of Jesus.

Verse 10: *When they saw the star, they were overjoyed.*

The Magi saw the star's reappearance as confirming their purpose. This recognition of God's guidance filled them with great joy. Their search had achieved success.

Verse 11: *On coming to the house, they saw the child with his mother Mary, and they bowed down and worshiped him. Then they opened their treasures and presented him with gifts of gold and of incense and of myrrh.*

Some time had elapsed since Jesus' birth, for the family had settled in a *house.* When the Magi found this residence, they *saw the child with his mother Mary.* Then they *bowed down and worshiped him.* The homage of these educated Gentiles indicated the fulfillment of some Old Testament passages (Ps. 72:10-11; Isa. 60:6). These verses may explain the later Christian tradition that these Magi were kings. The visitors also *opened their treasures and presented him with gifts. Treasures* probably means coffers or treasure boxes. When approaching a superior in the ancient East, bringing gifts had special importance. Some Bible students see the Magi's giving gifts as not merely honoring a civil ruler but worshiping God because the word for *presented* appears in connection with offerings to God.

The gifts used to honor the new King were usually associated with royalty. *Gold* was a precious metal prized for its beauty and value. *Incense* (frankincense) was a glittering, fragrant gum obtained by making incisions in the bark of several trees. *Myrrh*, used in embalming, came from a tree found in Arabia and other places. Both *incense* and *myrrh* were sweet-smelling spices and perfumes appropriate for expressing adoration and worship. The Old Testament mentions all of these gifts (Isa. 60:6; Song of Sol. 3:6). Such gifts reflected the Queen of Sheba's homage to Solomon (1 Kings 10:1-2). Both ancient and modern Bible scholars have seen symbolic value in these gifts: gold suggesting royalty; incense representing divinity; and myrrh symbolizing Christ's death and burial. Certainly the Magi would not have understood their gifts in this symbolic way. The three gifts were simply expensive and not uncommon presents. These gifts probably helped Joseph finance the family's months of exile in Egypt and settlement in Nazareth.

Verse 12: *And having been warned in a dream not to go back to Herod, they returned to their country by another route.*

Although the Magi may not have recognized Herod's purposes at first, God *warned* them *in a dream* not to return to this ruler. The cultural background of the Magi regularly featured revelation by dreams. God used their astrological and cultural backgrounds to communicate with them. This does not mean He endorsed their astrology. God met these individuals where they were because He cared for them. The Magi returned home *by another route* to avoid Jerusalem.

The Magi traveled a great distance at some expense to worship a new-born King unknown to them. As believers who know the Lord, we should purpose to worship God even when it seems inconvenient to do so and with a willingness to give of our resources. We can plan ways to celebrate Jesus' birth with joy and meaning.

5. Herod's Hatred (Matt. 2:3-8)

Verse 3: *When King Herod heard this he was disturbed, and all Jerusalem with him.*

In contrast with the Magi's desire to worship the King of the Jews, King Herod *was disturbed. Disturbed* is a strong word meaning in turmoil, terrified, or greatly agitated. Herod had an understandable concern: as a foreigner (Edomite) and a Roman appointee, he feared a rival who possessed a royal claim of the true Davidic dynasty. Because of his cruel, unpredictable ways, Herod also feared the country would welcome any rival of his. The people hated him. *All Jerusalem* joined him in his upset turmoil because they knew only too well what Herod could do when in a rage over having his security threatened. Any question like the Magi's could cause more cruelty from the sick Herod, whose paranoia had already led him to multiple murders. Some scholars, however, believe *all Jerusalem* refers primarily to the religious leaders of Israel who dominated the city. Herod had personally placed many of them in their positions. This verse hints at Jerusalem's later rejection of the true King of the Jews.

Verse 4: *When he had called together all the people's chief priests and teachers of the law, he asked them where the Christ was to be born.*

Herod could not answer the Magi's question without help. He had to ask the religious authorities where this King of the Jews was to be born. This revealed his own lack of Scripture knowledge. Evidently many people knew the answer to this question (see John 7:41-42). It also indicated how seriously Herod viewed this possible source of trouble. He *called together all* the *chief priests and teachers of the law.* This may refer to the Jewish Sanhedrin, the highest court of the Jews, or to an informal gathering of priests and scribes. *Chief priests* refers to the hierarchy made up of the current high priest, any who had formerly occupied this position, and a substantial number of other leading priests. A few aristocratic families had filled the office of high priest. Herod, contrary to the law, fairly frequently made changes in the high priesthood to suit himself. The priests were Sadducees.

The *teachers of the law* or scribes represented the second key group of religious leaders in Jerusalem. These men had inherited the old profession of copying Scripture, but they had developed into a class of teachers who were trained in interpreting and applying the Old Testament as well. Since the Jews based much of their civil law on the Old Testament and its interpretations, the scribes were also lawyers. Most of the scribes were Pharisees. The Sanhedrin contained both Sadducees and Pharisees, but the former had the majority. The two groups did not get along with each other, nor did they like Herod. Herod might have called both groups together to guard against being tricked.

The imperfect tense of *he asked them* suggests that Herod inquired repeatedly, probably of one and another of the leaders gathered together. He understood that the King of the Jews and the *Christ* were titles of the same expected person. He had evidently heard of this anticipated King. Herod desperately wanted to learn what the Jews really knew about the coming of the Messiah.

Verse 5: *"In Bethlehem in Judea," they replied, "for this is what the prophet has written:*

The Jewish leaders answered Herod's question from Micah 5:2, *in Bethlehem in Judea.* This was a small city approximately five miles south of Jerusalem. The leaders literally stated, "what stands written through the prophet." This suggests the authoritative and ruling force of the verse quoted. It also implies that the prophet acted as the intermediate agent and was not the ultimate source of what stood written. He spoke God's message.

Verse 6: *"'But you, Bethlehem in the land of Judah, are by no means least among the rulers of Judah; for out of you will come a ruler who will be the shepherd of my people Israel.'"*

As was commonly done, Matthew recorded Micah 5:2 in a free paraphrase; it does not appear exactly like the Hebrew text or the Septuagint (the Greek translation of the Old Testament). For instance, Matthew replaced the ancient name of Bethlehem Ephrathah with a phrase his readers would recognize, *in the land of Judah.* This distinguished it from the Bethlehem in Galilee. The addition of *by no means* reversed Micah's statement of Bethlehem's lowly status. In fact, the fulfillment of this prophecy transformed Bethlehem from a relatively insignificant town into a city of great honor.

Careful Jewish readers would have known that Matthew did not make a mistake in quoting the Scriptures but was offering an interpretative explanation. He quoted freely in order to point out the text's application. The Gospel writer used only the first part of the verse from Micah. The remainder left unquoted ("whose origins are from of old, from ancient times") suggested the prophet was referring to more than a mere mortal.

Matthew also introduced words from 2 Samuel 5:2 to make clear the status of Jesus as a son of David, born in the city of David, to rule like David over the people of God. This addition added another aspect to the work of the royal Messiah. He would not only rule but also **shepherd** the **people** of **Israel.** The Old Testament frequently used *shepherd* as an image of a ruler of God's people. Shepherding involved guiding, guarding, feeding, caring, and having a sense of compassion.

Verse 7: *Then Herod called the Magi secretly and found out from them the exact time the star had appeared.*

Herod did not allow the **Magi** to leave his presence before he had first **found out from them the exact time** when they first had seen **the star.** He held a secret meeting with them. This wicked ruler was already scheming to kill the small boys of Bethlehem (2:16).

Verse 8: *He sent them to Bethlehem and said, "Go and make careful search for the child. As soon as you find him, report to me, so that I too may go and worship him."*

Herod **sent** the Magi to **Bethlehem** with instructions to bring back any information about the child they discovered. He boldly lied about why he wanted them to **report** back to him: so he **too may go and worship** the newborn King. Herod had no intentions of worshiping the child. He had so much confidence in his success and in his hypocritical deception of the Magi that he sent no escort with them. Some scholars think Herod was too sly and ruthless to depend on the help of these foreigners. Instead, he would probably have sent his troops with them. Yet Herod had no reason to doubt that the Magi would return with the information he needed. The presence of soldiers with them would have risked their chances of locating the child.

Herod did not intend to worship Jesus. What do we purpose to do when we enter our church's worship center, especially during this Christmas season? Sadly, some people attend worship services for social or business purposes rather than for spiritual reasons. Let us search our hearts and examine our own motives. Let us celebrate Jesus' birth with genuine love and generous devotion.

FOR FURTHER STUDY

1. Read the article on "Magi" in the *Holman Bible Dictionary,* page 910.

2. See the section "Dates in Jesus' Life" in *The New Testament: Its Background and Message* by Thomas D. Lea (Nashville: Broadman and Holman Publishers, 1996), pages 90-92.

3. Read the Christmas narratives in Luke (1:26-56; 2:1-20) and compare with Matthew's account.

4. Read the article "Who Were the Magi?" in the Winter issue of *Biblical Illustrator.*

The Week of December 31

MAKING A DIFFERENCE

Background Passage: Acts 18:23—19:41
Lesson Passages: Acts 19:11-17,23-27

INTRODUCTION

For over a year protesters had marched on the sidewalks outside my daughter's elementary school. They carried posters denouncing the superintendent of our city's school district. They used a bullhorn to shout chants about inequality. These people frightened many children. Unfortunately, these students also began forming strong negative opinions against the racial group represented by the protesters. Finally, a group of clergymen intervened in an attempt to bring reconciliation between the school board and the protesters. One local Baptist pastor even walked with the protesters one morning. The involvement of the ministers made a difference in the anger-filled situation. Eventually the two sides met for a series of meetings and decided on actions to relieve the tensions and end the picketing.

This lesson relates the impact of Paul's ministry in Ephesus, particularly on those who practiced sorcery and worshiped idols. It emphasizes that Christians can make a positive difference in their world.

Acts 18:23—19:41

1. Apollos Learned and Taught (18:23-28)
2. Paul Witnessed to John's Disciples in Ephesus (19:1-7)
3. Paul Preached and Performed Miracles (19:8-12)
4. Christian Influence Grew (19:13-22)
5. Idol Industry Opposed Christianity (19:23-41)

THE BACKGROUND

Paul evidently began his third missionary journey alone. Luke did mention, however, various companions in travel in the course of the journey. The entire mission lasted about four or five years. Paul's mission tour featured a three-year ministry in Ephesus, the major metropolitan center of the region, approximately A.D. 53-56. He set up his base in the city and worked outward from there. In Paul's day Ephesus was the most populous city of Asia Minor. Rome had made Ephesus the capital of the province of Asia and allowed the city to exist as a free city-state, independently managing its own affairs.

Ephesus was on the western coast of Asia Minor at the mouth of the Cayster River. Silting from the Cayster left the city several miles inland by the first century. In 1044 B.C. Greeks from Athens conquered the region. The city later came under the control of Croesus of Lydia (560 B.C.), Persians (546 B.C.), Macedonians under Alexander the Great (334 B.C.), and Seleucid kings (281 B.C.). Ephesus felt the first Roman influence in 190 B.C. under the client-kings of Pergamum. Attalus III, the last of the Pergamum kings, willed the city to Rome at his death in 133 B.C.

Located on the main highway connecting the Aegean Sea with the rich trade routes in the East, Ephesus was the main commercial center of Asia. As a trade hub, Ephesus linked the Greco-Roman world of the West with the rich interior of eastern Asia Minor. As the chief commercial route by sea between Italy and the East, Ephesus offered two options for travel and trade further east: by sea along the south of Asia Minor to Syria and by land on a road from the city to southeastern Asia Minor. The economic interests of the city increased under Roman rule. Its great trade caused Ephesus to become rich and populous.

Ephesus was a center for the worship of Artemis, the Greek name for the Roman goddess Diana. The Artemision, the temple of this fertility goddess, was one of the Seven Wonders of the ancient world. It was the largest marble temple of the Greek world. From the time Greek settlers had arrived in Asia Minor, a cult to a mother goddess had existed. The Greeks eventually identified their Artemis with this Asian goddess. The ritual of the temple services consisted in sacrifices and ceremonial prostitution. Hundreds of cult officials served in the temple rituals.

The temple served also as a refuge for fugitives from justice and as a major bank for the area. For a period of about a month in the spring of each year there were special religious festivals in Ephesus connected with the worship of Artemis. Followers poured into the city from many provinces. The tourist and pilgrim trade associated with the temple and cult of Artemis brought much wealth to Ephesus. A rival to Corinth in moral corruption, Ephesus was also a center for the practice of sorcery and every form of black art.

THE LESSON PASSAGE

1. Apollos Learned and Taught (Acts 18:23-28)

Paul's third missionary journey led him first from Syrian Antioch to Galatia and Phrygia where he visited churches he had established. Paul wanted to begin a new work in Ephesus, but his interest for the new ministry did not lead him to neglect the old. He knew the importance of continued nurture of new converts. The apostle then headed toward Ephesus.

The Holy Spirit had prevented him from going there on an earlier occasion (Acts 16:6), and his first visit there had been short (18:19-21).

In Ephesus Priscilla and Aquila met an eloquent Jewish preacher named Apollos, a native of Alexandria. Alexandria was a strategic city of North Africa. Founded by and named for Alexander the Great in 332 B.C., it had a large Jewish community. In New Testament times it was the second largest city in the empire, surpassed only by Rome.

Apollos was "a learned man, with a thorough knowledge of the Scriptures." He had received instruction in the "way of the Lord." The source of Apollos's instruction is not given. Perhaps Egyptians from Alexandria were among those converted in Jerusalem on the day of Pentecost, bringing home with them the gospel message. What Apollos knew, he knew well. When he came to Ephesus to preach, he must have created quite a stir because of his power and skill in communication. Nevertheless, his message revealed only partial understanding. Although he taught accurately the things concerning Jesus, he knew only the baptism of John.

How could Apollos know so much and yet so little? Communication in that day traveled slowly and with great difficulty. Apollos could have believed in Jesus as the Messiah without knowing much about His life and ministry. Thus, he knew about John's baptism of repentance, anticipation, and preparation. No one had told him of Jesus' baptism as a testimony of fulfillment and as a living symbol of the resurrection.

Priscilla and Aquila heard him and recognized gaps in his understanding. Rather than publicly rebuke him for his ignorance, they took him aside, invited him to their home, and explained the way of God more accurately. Apollos had a teachable spirit and became an even more effective proclaimer of the gospel. When he wanted to go to the province of Achaia to preach, Priscilla, Aquila, and others in the Ephesian fellowship encouraged him. They probably also helped him with funds and gave him a letter of introduction to Christian groups already at work in Achaia. The mention of the Ephesian brothers who provided Apollos with a letter of recommendation gives clear evidence that a church had been established in Ephesus before Paul arrived. The believers in Achaia welcomed Apollos. This gifted speaker powerfully demonstrated by the Scriptures that Jesus is the Christ. He justified the confidence the Ephesian believers had placed in him.

2. Paul Witnessed to John's Disciples in Ephesus (Acts 19:1-7)

After Apollos left to minister in Corinth, Paul went to Ephesus, where he found "some disciples." He asked them if they had received the Holy Spirit when they believed. They replied that they had not heard about the

"Holy Spirit." They had received only "John's baptism."

Were these 12 men Christians? Some Bible students believe the description of them as "disciples" implies that they were. Luke commonly used this term for Christians. On the other hand, their answer to Paul's question and his response implied that they had never been saved. Apollos, who had experienced John's baptism, was apparently not rebaptized; but these people were. This group did not know the gospel. They knew only John's message of preparation. Perhaps they did not even understand this well since Paul explained the meaning of John's baptism (19:4). They failed to recognize Jesus as the One whom John had proclaimed as the promised Messiah. Yet, their experience with John had prepared them well. They immediately responded with faith to Paul's good news that Jesus Christ had come, and they were baptized in His name. This represents the only instance of rebaptism in the New Testament. When Paul laid his hands on them, the Holy Spirit came upon them. They began speaking with tongues and prophesying.

3. Paul Preached and Performed Miracles (Acts 19:8-12)

Paul wrote his letters to the church at Corinth during his extended stay in Ephesus. In that correspondence he spoke of difficulties he encountered in Asia. Some of his worries arose from the conditions in the Corinthian church that others had reported to him. Acts does not speak of these problems in Achaia. He only mentioned two areas of trouble in Ephesus—the Jewish opposition and the incident caused by the silversmith, Demetrius. Acts summarizes Paul's Ephesian ministry in terms of of his preaching (19:8-10) and his miracles (19:11-12).

For three months Paul ministered in the synagogue in Ephesus, preaching fearlessly to the Jews concerning the kingdom of God. Some Jews rejected Paul's message so strongly that they began to speak evil of the Way publicly. Consequently, Paul turned from them and took with him those who had become disciples. He moved to a nearby lecture hall owned by a man named Tyrannus. For two years he preached the gospel there. During this time the gospel spread "so that all the Jews and Greeks who lived in the province of Asia heard the word of the Lord" (19:10).

Verse 11: *God did extraordinary miracles through Paul,*

Paul's ministry in Ephesus also involved healings and exorcisms God worked through him. The apostle himself referred to the signs, wonders, and miracles that accompanied his ministry (2 Cor. 12:12; Rom. 15:19). Luke described these as *extraordinary miracles*. He spoke of unusual works of power directly *through Paul.* The Greek text literally reads "through the hands of Paul."

Verse 12: *so that even handkerchiefs and aprons that had touched him* *were taken to the sick, and their illnesses were cured and the evil spirits left them.*

Luke also related indirect miracles. The people would take cloths Paul had touched and carry them *to the sick* or demon-possessed for healing. *Handkerchiefs* likely refers to a face cloth used for wiping perspiration, corresponding somewhat to the modern handkerchief. It could also refer to sweat bands tied around the head. *Aprons* refers to a workman's apron that persons tied around the waist. The people believed that even personal garments such as items Paul used in the trade of tentmaking and leather working had the ability to heal. The New Testament refers to other miracles with this same unusual character of power: the hem of Jesus' garment (Mark 5:25-34; 6:56) and the shadow of Peter (Acts 5:15).

Ephesus was the center of all sorts of magic and superstition. The term "Ephesian writings" was commonly used in antiquity to refer to documents containing spells and magical formulas. Luke criticized pagan magic practices yet described here similar magical beliefs in a Christianized form that proved effective in the apostle's ministry. Paul met his audiences at a point of common ground in their beliefs to lead them to the good news of salvation in Christ. At Ephesus he did the same in the working of miracles. Of course, the *handkerchiefs* and *aprons* had no magical power. The actual power lay in God through the faith of the recipients. God is the source of all physical and spiritual healing in keeping with His larger purposes. He also can accommodate Himself to the mind-set of the people in any age. The apostles' miracles did not serve as ends in themselves. They always led to opportunities for faith and commitment. The power of God manifested in Paul's miracles ultimately led to the Ephesians' overcoming their magic, evil, and superstition.

God performed miracles through Paul that resulted in people being healed physically and spiritually. We can make a difference in broken lives by ministering to the physical as well as the spiritual needs of others. Meeting physical needs can lead to opportunities for sharing the gospel of Jesus Christ.

4. Christian Influence Grew (Acts 19:13-22)

Verse 13: *Some Jews who went around driving out evil spirits tried to invoke the name of the Lord Jesus over those who were demon-possessed. They would say, "In the name of Jesus, whom Paul preaches, I command you to come out."*

In Paul's day certain individuals **went around** making a living by claiming to have various powers. Magicians and charlatans seemed present everywhere in the culture. They offered cures and blessings by their spells and incantations, charging a fee for their services. They readily called on the names of any and every god or divinity in their "prayers." Often they recited long lists of names to make sure they included the right god in any particular case.

Pagans even used the various Jewish names of God. A magical formula preserved in an ancient magical papyrus reads, "I adjure thee by the God of the Hebrews, Jesus." In the Greco-Roman world Jewish exorcists enjoyed high respect. Since many exorcists knew that the Jews' reverence led them not to pronounce God's name, the exorcists assumed that meant His name had special magic. They highly esteemed those in the Jewish priesthood, assuming the priests were most likely to know the true pronunciation of the divine name and thus most able to release its power.

Many people observed Paul's miracles. Some sought his help for healing from their own illnesses and demon possession. Others, however, coveted his power and began to imitate him. Among these were a group of wandering Jewish exorcists. They had observed how Paul drove out *evil spirits* by invoking the *name of Jesus,* and they attempted to do the same themselves. Since Paul's "spell" using Jesus' name seemed to work for him, they too would give it a try.

Verse 14: *Seven sons of Sceva, a Jewish chief priest, were doing this.*

A first-century Jewish historian, Josephus, listed all the names of the Jewish chief (also translated "high") priests up to the fall of the temple. He did not include a *Sceva.* Possibly *Sceva* actually belonged to one of the families of the high priests. Probably, however, he assumed the title *chief priest* for professional purposes in order to enhance his sons' reputations and to impress their clients. Thinking Sceva was a high priest, the only one who could enter the holy of holies and thus have close contact with the Divine, people might conclude he had extraordinary powers to practice the magical arts. Sceva and his sons no doubt deceived others to make their business of driving out evil spirits more profitable.

Verse 15: *[One day] the evil spirit answered them, "Jesus I know, and I know about Paul, but who are you?"*

When the Jewish exorcists attempted to use Jesus' name, the *evil spirit* in the man whom they were trying to cure challenged their right to use it. The targeted demon confessed to knowing *Jesus* and *Paul.* In the exorcisms Jesus performed, the demons often confessed Him. Now this one even acknowledged that the power of Jesus worked through Paul. *But who are you?* What right did these men have to act in the name of Jesus?

Verse 16: *Then the man who had the evil spirit jumped on them and overpowered them all. He gave them such a beating that they ran out of the house naked and bleeding.*

When Sceva's sons tried to use Jesus' name in their exorcisms, these seven exorcists found they were dealing with realities far beyond their ability to cope. Under demonic influence, the man turned violently on the seven and *overpowered them all.* He *gave them such a beating* that all seven *ran* for their lives *out of the house naked and bleeding.*

An extreme sense of modesty characterized Judaism. Consequently, the nakedness of the Jewish exorcists symbolized their total humiliation. They learned a lesson about the danger of using the name of Jesus in their dabbling in the spiritual realm. They learned Christianity has nothing to do with magic. The name of Jesus is not a magical formula. The power of Jesus could drive out the demonic, but His Spirit would only work through those who, like Paul, confessed and followed Him.

Verse 17: *When this became known to the Jews and Greeks living in Ephesus, they were all seized with fear, and the name of the Lord Jesus was held in high honor.*

News of what happened spread quickly through Ephesus *to the Jews and Greeks.* A reverent fear seized them, and they magnified the name of the Lord Jesus, holding it *in high honor.* In this setting where superstition influenced the people, showing the superiority of Jesus' power to that of demons helped spread the Christian faith. Those who came to believe in Jesus still might have been tempted to think of His power and Person in ways related to magic, yet God's work in their lives would continue to purify them of such pagan thinking.

From this incident the Ephesians learned negatively not to misuse the name of Jesus or treat it lightly, for it is a powerful name. Positively, many Christians renounced their secret acts of magic, and pagans who had practiced sorcery came to believe. As mentioned previously, Ephesus had a reputation as a center for magic. The famous statue of Artemis had mysterious terms engraved on her crown, girdle, and feet. People believed these "Ephesian scripts" had great power. The Ephesian Christians now openly forsook such practices. They wanted to demonstrate the change in their lives for all to see. Those who abandoned their magic did so with some personal sacrifice. Books of any kind were expensive in those days, but books of magic commanded a great price. The complete repentance of these magicians led to the burning of thousands of dollars' worth of magic books in a public bonfire. What a testimony this served to those who witnessed this event!

Acts 19:20 summarizes Paul's Ephesian ministry: "the word of the Lord spread widely and grew in power." Paul decided to conclude his mission in the East and move farther west toward Rome. He explained that he first must go to Jerusalem to deliver the collection for the Jerusalem Christians (Rom. 15:25-32). In the meantime he sent two helpers to Macedonia to strengthen the churches while he stayed a little longer in the province of Asia.

How do we use Jesus' name? We are to honor the name of Jesus and follow Him in faith rather than use His name to exploit others. The power to change other people comes from Christ. We cannot use that power by reciting Jesus' name like a magic charm. God works His power only through those whom He chooses.

5. Idol Industry Opposed Christianity (Acts 19:23-41)

The willingness of the Ephesian Christians to sacrifice financially for their faith contrasted to the greed of the pagan craftsmen of Ephesus. The latter saw Paul's witness as threatening their economic survival. The rest of Acts 19 is about their public demonstration against the apostle: the starting of the riot by Demetrius (19:23-27), the uproar in the theater (19:28-34), and the calming of the crowd by the city clerk (19:35-41). The situation might have held more danger than Acts taken alone suggests. In what may well be allusions to this riot, Paul wrote later that he had fought wild beasts in Ephesus (1 Cor. 15:32), had despaired even of life in the face of a deadly peril in Asia (2 Cor. 1:8-11), and that Priscilla and Aquila had risked their lives for him (Rom. 16:3-4).

Verse 23: *About that time there arose a great disturbance about the Way.*

The riot sparked by Demetrius took place toward the end of Paul's stay in Ephesus when he already was making plans for his departure. Luke described this **great disturbance** as being **about the Way.** He used *the Way* to show that the opposition was not merely against Paul. Primarily it threatened the gospel and its continued outreach. Only Acts refers to Christians as those of the *Way.* Throughout the Ephesian narrative Luke used this term. Priscilla and Aquila explained *the Way* more fully to Apollos (18:26). Some of the Jews in the Ephesian synagogue spoke against *the Way* (19:9). Now a new resistance to *the Way* arose from worshipers of Artemis. Basically the term means Christianity. Behind the *the Way* lies the concepts of the "way of the Lord" or God in Christ as the "way of salvation." God has appointed the way of life for people to follow for salvation. Jesus declared that He is the Way (John 14:6).

Verse 24: *A silversmith named Demetrius, who made silver shrines of Artemis, brought in no little business for the craftsmen.*

Demetrius was behind the whole incident of opposition. He was making a good living by the manufacture of **silver shrines of Artemis.** This could refer to miniature silver replicas of the Artemis temple or silver statues of Artemis herself. Cult followers used these things as souvenirs, offerings, and charms. The sale of these small silver items brought great profit to the silversmiths. Paul's preaching had turned many away from the idolatry of the Artemis cult. The fall in the demand for their products alarmed these tradesmen. The Ephesian silversmiths probably regarded their trade guild as being under the special patronage of Artemis, in whose honor they made so many of their products.

Verse 25: *He called them together, along with the workmen in related trades, and said: "Men, you know we receive a good income from this business.*

Demetrius organized a protest demonstration. He knew what would influence his fellow tradesmen, so he put before them the real issue: **We receive a good income from this business.** Demetrius's real concern centered on the damage Paul's preaching was doing to his business. Yet as a skilled speaker and motivator, he would soon mix business and religion in his appeal to his fellow craftsmen (19:27). He understood that religion and patriotism would more likely get the public's attention. He probably hoped to turn the people against the missionaries and stir up greater devotion for the goddess Artemis. Greater loyalty to her would result in greater profits for him.

Verse 26: *And you see and hear how this fellow Paul has convinced and led astray large numbers of people here in Ephesus and in practically the whole province of Asia. He says that man-made gods are no gods at all.*

Demetrius then correctly blamed **this fellow Paul** for causing all the trouble. He said Paul had **convinced and led astray** crowds of **people** in the city and throughout the province. The word translated *led astray* literally means seduced. Paul's denying that idols were real gods was viewed as contrary to fact. (See Paul's Areopagus speech, 17:29.) Those who turned to Christ and no longer believed in idols made by human hands were viewed as deceived.

Verse 27: *There is danger not only that our trade will lose its good name, but also that the temple of the great goddess Artemis will be discredited, and the goddess herself, who is worshiped throughout the province of Asia and the world, will be robbed of her divine majesty."*

Not only did Demetrius make a rational argument against Paul, but he also appealed to the emotions of his listeners and broadened his appeal to the wider public. The ordinary people might not care that Demetrius was going out of business, but they would care if the temple of Artemis lost its popularity or if the goddess who drew worshipers to Ephesus from all over the world lost her importance. Demetrius accused Paul of giving the silversmiths' business a bad **name** for promoting idolatry. He also accused the apostle of endangering the religion of Ephesus by discrediting the reputation of **Artemis** and robbing her of **her divine majesty.** In referring to this cult being spread **throughout** the whole **world,** he indirectly appealed to civic pride. To attack *Artemis* was to attack Ephesus.

Demetrius's argument had a basis in reality. Paul preached forcefully against idolatry. His message presented a threat to anyone who made a living from idols as well as the Artemis cult. The immoral practices in which followers of Artemis engaged opposed the gospel's call to holy living. Yet Demetrius really opposed Paul not for religious reasons but because Paul affected his bank account. The gospel becomes most controversial when it conflicts with economic interests.

Demetrius's appeal caused the money-hungry craftsmen to run forth and shout, "Great is Artemis of the Ephesians!" A full-blown riot soon followed. The angry mob dragged two of Paul's Macedonian companions, Gaius and Aristarchus, into the great theater of Ephesus. Paul wanted to enter the theater to defend his associates. Paul's friends, both Christians as well as pagan officials, persuaded him not to do so because they feared for his safety. That some of the officials of the province tried to protect Paul showed that his fellow Roman citizens respected him.

The scene was one of utter confusion, some shouting one thing, some another. Most people had merely given in to a mob mentality and did not know what was going on. The Jews pushed forward Alexander, a leader in their community, to let the crowd know that they had done nothing to threaten Artemis. When the crowd realized he was Jewish, they only shouted him down with the chant "Great is Artemis of the Ephesians!"

Finally, the town clerk, the chief administrative official of the free-city of Ephesus, was able to quiet the wild crowd. He assured his unruly hearers that everyone acknowledged that Ephesus was the guardian of the temple of Artemis. He pointed out the innocence of the two Christians whom they had seized. He then urged Demetrius and his fellow craftsmen to take whatever charges they had against Paul and his companions to the courts or the assembly. He warned them that Rome would not tolerate such behavior, fearing it would lead to open rebellion against the empire. The wise counsel of this respected official finally calmed the crowd. He dismissed the gathering, and the people dispersed.

Like Paul, we can expect conflict whenever our witness impacts people's pocketbooks or the influence of another belief system. We should realize that making a difference in the world for the sake of Jesus may bring us enemies or difficulties. We cannot use such opposition as an excuse for failing to present the claims of Christ. We must remain faithful in this task. God will help us and make us adequate for ministry.

FOR FURTHER STUDY

1. See the following articles in *Biblical Illustrator:* "The Ephesian Church," Winter 1996; "A History of Ephesus," Summer 2000; "The Third Missionary Journey" and "Aristarchus," Winter 2000.

2. Read the article on "Ephesus" in the *Holman Bible Dictionary*, page 424.

The Week of January 7

SETTING AN EXAMPLE

Background Passage: Acts 20:1-38
Lesson Passages: Acts 20:17-24,33-35

INTRODUCTION

Lately I attended the funeral of a seminary colleague. The service both celebrated the life of this man and glorified God. This professor had an exemplary character. He modeled kindness, helpfulness, and humility. As cancer attacked his body the last four years of his life, he showed others how to persevere in serving God despite personal pain and problems. His son shared that even during his final days in a hospital bed this teacher witnessed to a nurse who professed belief in nothing. In sermons preached while undergoing cancer therapy, this man stated that God had a purpose in his life. He expressed a desire to live; but if God wanted him home, he was ready to go. He desired to glorify God above all. He set a Christian example for his family, friends, students, and fellow teachers.

This lesson focuses on Paul's farewell statement to the Ephesian church elders. From it we learn about the example Paul had set for the believers in Ephesus as he ministered among them. The apostle's life challenges us to determine to set a Christian example for others.

Acts 20:1-38

1. Paul's Travels to Troas (20:1-6)
2. Paul's All-Night Speaking at Troas (20:7-12)
3. Paul's Brief Journey to Miletus (20:13-16)
4. Paul's Farewell Address to the Ephesian Elders (20:17-38)

THE BACKGROUND

Acts provides three examples of Paul's messages given during the course of his missionary work. The first was delivered to a Jewish audience in the synagogue at Pisidian Antioch during his first mission trip (Acts 13:16-41). On his second mission trip, Paul delivered a message to a Gentile audience before the Areopagus at Athens (17:22-31). Bible students often identify the third message as Paul's farewell address to the Ephesian elders (20:17-38). He delivered this discourse at Miletus in the course of his third missionary journey. In his other speeches as well as his five defenses (chaps. 22—26), Paul addressed non-Christian audiences. The farewell address at Miletus, of course, was given to believers.

Of all the apostle's speeches in Acts, the Miletus address to the Ephesian church's leaders has the most in common with his letters because Paul was addressing Christians. In his letters Paul encouraged, warned, and exhorted his converts. He did the same in this farewell.

The apostle consciously thought of this address as his final legacy to the leaders of the Ephesian church. He did not expect to return. As a parting speech, Paul's words have much in common with similar speeches in both Old and New Testaments, such as Jacob's blessing to his sons (Gen. 49), Joshua's farewell address to Israel (Josh. 23—24), and Samuel's good-by to the nation of Israel (1 Sam. 12). Jesus' words to His disciples at the Last Supper provide a New Testament example. Perhaps the closest parallel to the Miletus speech in Paul's letters can be found in 1 Timothy 4:1-16 and 2 Timothy 3:1—4:8.

THE LESSON PASSAGE

1. Paul's Travels to Troas (Acts 20:1-6)

When the uproar from the riot started by the craftsmen had settled, Paul called together the disciples in Ephesus to encourage them to remain faithful. He then traveled through Macedonia, encouraging believers. The apostle finally arrived in Greece, probably settling in Corinth. This was Paul's final visit to Corinth, and it lasted three months. This probably was during the winter months (when travel was most difficult) A.D. 55-56. Many Bible students believe Paul wrote his epistle to the Romans during this time. While strengthening the believers in Corinth and writing, Paul also coordinated the collection of the offering he wanted to take to Jerusalem to relieve the suffering of the Jewish Christians there.

With Paul carrying a substantial amount of money collected from the Gentile churches, he undoubtedly wanted to get to Jerusalem as quickly and safely as possible. As he was about to board a ship for Syria, the apostle and his friends uncovered a plot on his life. Paul changed his plans, journeyed by land to Macedonia, and sailed from Philippi.

Paul had gathered traveling companions to serve as delegates from the Gentile churches. They joined Paul both for protection and as official representatives of the churches. These men were from each of the major areas where Paul had established work. Sopater, Aristarchus, and Secundus came from the Macedonian churches. Gaius and Timothy represented the churches of southern Galatia. Tychicus and Trophimus were the delegates from the church of Asia. These Gentile believers would share in the presentation of the collected offering and give the Jewish Christians in Jerusalem further exposure to their Gentile brothers in Christ. At the same time, these Gentiles would have a chance to meet

Jewish Christians, see how they lived under persecution, and worship in the Gentile court of the Herodian temple, which reflected much of their spiritual heritage.

Paul and his friends traveled to Philippi. The traveling companions went on ahead of the apostle to wait for him in Troas. At this point in the account Luke resumed the use of "we." This first-person plural narrative last occurred in the account of Paul's Philippian ministry (Acts 16:16-17). This may indicate that Luke had stayed in Philippi and ministered there until this point. Paul and Luke remained in Philippi until after the Passover before setting sail to meet the others in Troas. The group stayed for seven days in Troas in final preparation for their trip to Jerusalem.

2. Paul's All-Night Speaking at Troas (Acts 20:7-12)

Paul and his companions spent a week in Troas, evidently awaiting the departure of their ship. On Sunday, their last day there, Paul met with the believers for worship. This is one of the earliest references to Christians meeting for worship on the "first day of the week" or Sunday (20:7). For Jewish Christians the Sabbath remained a sacred day. Gentile Christians, to whom the Sabbath was just another day, remembered the Lord on the day of His resurrection. Eventually Sunday became the only day of worship. The breaking of bread referred to the love feast, a fellowship meal that included the Lord's Supper. Since he was leaving the next morning, Paul spent all the time he could with the Christians in Troas, talking until midnight. Believers met in the evening, probably the most convenient time because most of them worked during the day.

Eutychus sat in the window of the upstairs room where they were meeting. "Young man" usually referred to a boy of 8-14 years (20:9). The combination of the late hour, the long speech, the heat, the smoke from the torches or lamps (suggesting a lack of oxygen and the hypnotic effect of flickering flames) proved too much for Eutychus. He dozed off, lost his balance, and fell to the ground from the third floor window. The fall evidently killed him and brought the meeting to a sudden, shocking halt. In an action similar to that of Elijah and Elisha (1 Kings 17:21; 2 Kings 4:34-35), Paul threw himself on the young man and put his arms around him. God restored Eutychus to life. This miracle served as a vivid reminder to the Christians at Troas that Jesus, whom Paul had been preaching, is indeed the resurrection and the life. Assured of the youth's recovery, the people reassembled in the hall, broke bread together, and Paul picked up where he had left off. The apostle continued in his discourse with them until daybreak. Afterward he departed for Assos to catch his ship. Eutychus returned home fully recovered.

The evening had great significance for the church at Troas. Paul had taught them. They had experienced fellowship in the Lord's Supper and had witnessed a dramatic sign of God's presence and power. What they had seen, heard, and done that night encouraged and strengthened their faith.

3. Paul's Brief Journey to Miletus (Acts 20:13-16)

Because of the geography of that part of the world, Paul could walk just about as fast as the ship could sail from Troas to Assos. So he chose to go by foot to Assos, a trip of about 20 miles, while his traveling companions sailed with the ship. The boat had to go around Cape Lectum to reach Assos, making the sea route longer and more difficult than the land route. At Assos Paul boarded the ship that was skirting the shoreline, putting in at major towns and cities along the route. Attempting to reach Jerusalem by Pentecost, Paul decided not to go all the way to Ephesus. This would enable him to escape the emotional strain of another parting with the entire Ephesian church and avoid some local danger.

4. Paul's Farewell Address to the Ephesian Elders (Acts 20:17-38)

The body of the Miletus address has three parts: (1) Paul's past example in ministering at Ephesus (20:18-21); (2) Paul's following God's leadership to go to Jerusalem in spite of dangers (20:22-24); and (3) admonitions and warnings about what the church at Ephesus would face in the future (20:25-31). Paul added a blessing (20:32) and then gave further words of exhortation, directing his hearers to follow his example and the teachings of Jesus (20:33-35).

Verse 17: *From Miletus, Paul sent to Ephesus for the elders of the church.*

At **Miletus** the ship docked for a number of days to load and unload cargo. While the ship remained in harbor, Paul **sent** a message to **Ephesus,** some 30 miles away, asking **the elders of the church** in that city to come and see him.

The word *elders* literally refers to older people but is used to designate those with the maturity to lead. Here it indicates church leaders. In 20:28 Paul also called them "overseers" and "shepherds" of the church. We do not know much about local church organization at this point in church history. These elders could have been appointed by the missionaries and confirmed by the church (see 14:23 for that practice). The Miletus elders promptly responded to Paul's invitation.

Verse 18: *When they arrived, he said to them: "You know how I lived the whole time I was with you, from the first day I came into the province of Asia.*

Paul began his address by reminding the elders how he had conducted himself during the **whole time** of his ministry with them, **from the first day** he entered the **province of Asia.** Evidently Paul's Ephesian opponents had been speaking against him in his absence. He defended his conduct and teaching by appealing to his hearers' personal knowledge of him and describing the basic characteristics of his ministry. In so doing, he reminded them of the example he had set in Christian living and service.

Verse 19: *I served the Lord with great humility and with tears, although I was severely tested by the plots of the Jews.*

Paul described his work in Asia as serving **the Lord.** He also identified himself as a servant or bond slave of Christ (Rom. 1:1; Gal. 1:10; Phil. 1:1). For the apostle, the idea of service had priority over any thought of the status that might belong to the servant. Consequently, the first characteristic of his ministry he singled out for mention was **humility,** lowliness of mind. Paul did not hold himself above or apart from anyone. *Humility* is the proper attitude of a servant. Perhaps his humility strongly contrasted with his enemies' arrogance.

Second, Paul carried out his ministry with **tears.** This expressed his personal concern for those to whom he ministered.

Third, by reminding the Ephesian elders that he **was severely tested by the plots of the Jews,** Paul implied the patience and perseverance with which he continued his work. The constant Jewish persecution probably tempted him at times to give up. Acts does not relate any specific Jewish plot against Paul in Ephesus, though such plots occurred frequently in Paul's work—at Pisidian Antioch, Iconium, Lystra, Thessalonica, Berea, and Corinth. The most recent plot by the Jews had caused the apostle's presence at Miletus at this time, making him change his original plan to sail directly to Syria from Corinth.

We too can set a Christian example for others by serving the Lord with humility and concern for others, persevering despite any opposition.

Verse 20: *You know that I have not hesitated to preach anything that would be helpful to you but have taught you publicly and from house to house.*

Paul had not withheld any teachings that would prove **helpful** or profitable for his hearers, even those things they might not have welcomed. He reminded the elders of the honesty and openness of his own preaching. He had preached both **publicly and from house to house.** *Publicly* referred to Paul's preaching in the synagogue at Ephesus and the lecture hall of Tyrannus (Acts 19:8-10). The reference to houses most likely meant the house-church meetings of the Ephesian Christians. The apostle emphasized this point so strongly that some students believe he was replying to some criticism. Acts does not record any such accusations of Paul at Ephesus, but Paul warned the Ephesian leaders later in his speech that false teachers would arise to trouble their church.

Verse 21: *I have declared to both Jews and Greeks that they must turn to God in repentance and have faith in our Lord Jesus.*

Finally, Paul emphasized the inclusiveness of his ministry. He had preached to everyone, **both Jews and Greeks.** He did not leave out anyone. In Ephesus as elsewhere the apostle had begun his preaching in the synagogue, leaving it only when the Jews refused to listen. Then he turned to the Gentiles. Paul's special calling was to be an apostle to the Gentiles, but he never gave up on his own people.

Paul's preaching focused on **repentance** and **faith in our Lord Jesus.** To repent means to turn from one's former life **to God.** The gospel includes *repentance* and *faith,* believing or placing one's trust in Jesus. Paul rooted his ministry in this gospel.

We can follow Paul's pattern of ministry in our own lives by sharing the gospel wherever and to whomever we have an opportunity.

Verse 22: *"And now, compelled by the Spirit, I am going to Jerusalem, not knowing what will happen to me there.*

After reminding the Ephesian leaders of the character of his ministry, Paul now prepared them for his absence. The apostle was on his way **to Jerusalem.** He described this journey in two ways. First, it was a journey of necessity—the Holy Spirit **compelled** him. Paul knew that God was guiding him to go. He, therefore, had to obey. Paul evidently had sensed this guidance and decided to take this course while still in Ephesus (19:21). The completion of his ministry involved taking to the Jerusalem church the money sent by Gentile believers in Galatia, Macedonia, Achaia, and Asia. He viewed this collection as a tangible symbol of the faith of these Gentiles and of the unity Jews and Gentiles share in Christ.

Second, the journey to Jerusalem was a journey of uncertainty. He did not know **what** would **happen** to him **there.** Paul reflected something of this uncertainty in his appeal for prayer that he might be delivered from danger in Jerusalem and that the church there would receive the gift gratefully (Rom. 15:30-32). These requests indicated Paul's serious misgivings about how the Jerusalem believers would receive the relief offering as well as an awareness that going there involved some personal risk.

Verse 23: *I only know that in every city the Holy Spirit warns me that prison and hardships are facing me.*

The **Holy Spirit** not only gave Paul direction, but He also warned him. Paul did **know** this with certainty—**in every city . . . prison and hardships** awaited him. This could mean that in every city along the way the Spirit prophesied persecution in Jerusalem or in every city Paul visited he would face suffering. Luke probably meant the former. God gave some of these warnings through Christian prophets (Acts 21:4,11). Perhaps some warnings came through personal revelations to Paul.

Some people might see the activity of the Spirit as contradictory here. On the one hand, the Holy Spirit compelled Paul to Jerusalem. On the other hand, He warned the apostle of the extreme risk in going there. These messages of the Spirit are not contradictory. God led Paul to Jerusalem, for He had a purpose for Paul's going there. The warnings prepared Paul for what he would face there. The warnings also assured him that whatever happened, God was in it. Paul would experience severe trials, but through them he ultimately would bear his witness in Rome itself, the heart of the empire.

Verse 24: *However, I consider my life worth nothing to me, if only I may finish the race and complete the task the Lord Jesus has given me—the task of testifying to the gospel of God's grace.*

Paul shared the reason he was willing to face the dangers in Jerusalem. He considered his own *life worth nothing* to himself. He did not know whether his suffering would lead to his death, but he emphasized that he was prepared for that possibility. He did not regard his own life as a precious possession to be held on to at all costs. In his letters Paul often stated his attitude of readiness to suffer, even to die, for Christ (Phil. 1:19-26). What mattered most to Paul was that he would *finish the race and complete the task the Lord Jesus* had *given* him. He frequently described his ministry as running a footrace. He had received this ministry from Jesus at his conversion and described it as the task of *testifying to the gospel of God's grace.* Although this exact phrase never occurs in his letters, it summarizes the heart of Paul's message.

Paul had a commitment to fulfill God's purpose for his life. We can set a Christian example for others by committing to achieve God's purpose for our lives. What does God want us to do?

Paul gave his farewell to the Ephesian elders because they would never see him again. He emphasized that he had done his part faithfully, proclaiming the "whole will of God" (Acts 20:27). Therefore, he was "innocent of the blood of all" people (v. 26). The apostle's words reflected the "watchman" image of Ezekiel 33:1-16. The watchman fulfilled his job when he blew the warning trumpet in the face of danger. Once he had sounded his warning, he no longer had responsibility for the lives of those he had warned. Paul had preached the full gospel and called people to repentance. They were responsible for what they did with that message.

The address continued with a warning of coming persecution from outside the Ephesian church and apostasy from within. The apostle first exhorted the elders to guard themselves and "all the flock of which the Holy Spirit" had made them "overseers" (Acts 20:28). "Overseer," often translated *bishop,* did not refer to a monarchical bishop ruling over a number of congregations. This kind of organization did not develop until the second century. The New Testament writers often interchanged the term "overseer" with the term "elder." Acts 20:17 describes the Ephesian leaders as "elders." The term "overseer" in 20:28 was used probably to describe their function, that of overseeing the church. The Holy Spirit gifted these leaders for this responsibility.

Paul described the church as a "flock" (20:28), a familiar Old Testament metaphor for God's people. The New Testament applies the image to the church and its leaders (1 Pet. 5:2). Following this image the apostle commanded the elders to be shepherds of the church of God. They were to care for God's people. The church belongs to God because He bought it. The cost of redemption was Jesus' blood, the blood of God's own Son (Acts 20:28). Paul continued the shepherd imagery by warning the Ephesian elders of a time to come when false teachers would assault the flock of God. They would come both from outside ("savage wolves," 20:29) and inside the church. In the face of such danger church leaders constantly must be alert, as shepherds keeping awake to watch for attacking wolves at night.

Paul committed the leaders to the word of God's grace. He knew the truth of the gospel could build them up and give them an inheritance (eternal life) among all those who are sanctified, those who have been set apart as God's people in Christ. Paul wanted the Ephesian elders to continue to lead the church after his departure, urging them above all to be faithful to the gospel in the light of the coming threats.

Verse 33: *I have not coveted anyone's silver or gold or clothing.*

Paul made one last appeal concerning an important matter of personal conduct. He pled with his hearers to follow his own example of selfless giving. He could truthfully say that he had not *coveted* any material wealth or goods. *Silver, gold,* and fine *clothing* represented wealth and status symbols in the ancient world. Paul had not looked for material reward for his pastoral labors. He urged the elders of the Ephesian church to care for the needs of God's people in the same way. The apostle never used his ministry as a mask to cover up greed (1 Thess. 2:5).

Verse 34: *You yourselves know that these hands of mine have supplied my own needs and the needs of my companions.*

At Corinth and Thessalonica Paul supported himself with his own hands in his tentmaking (Acts 18:3; 1 Thess. 2:9). He followed the same pattern of self-support at Ephesus. Having no wealth of his own, he found contentment in working with his own *hands* to support himself, although as an apostle he might have claimed support from the churches. He expressed gratitude for gifts from the churches (Phil. 4:10-19), yet almost seemed to have been embarrassed by them. Such gifts from existing churches together with his own work enabled him to avoid being a burden to the churches in which he currently was working. In his letters Paul exhorted his fellow Christians to follow his example and work with their own hands instead of depending on others (1 Thess. 4:11).

Verse 35: *In everything I did, I showed you that by this kind of hard work we must help the weak, remembering the words the Lord Jesus himself said: 'It is more blessed to give than to receive.' "*

The apostle gave the additional motivation that such **hard work** enabled a person to help the **weak.** To support his exhortation, he called on the Ephesian elders to remember the words of Jesus: *It is more blessed to give than to receive.* This means that persons who can do so should give to help others rather than simply gather further wealth for themselves. Evidently greed among church leaders was a real problem in Asia Minor. It particularly marked the false teachers. Paul insisted that freedom from the love of money was a major qualification for church leaders. Ministers must serve and give, not take. Those who lead the flock of God should focus on the needs of others and have more concern with giving than with acquiring. Paul often related his ethical exhortations to the teachings of Jesus and the personal example of Jesus. He did so here. The words he quoted from Jesus do not appear in any of the Gospels, but they closely parallel Luke 6:38. Jesus' actions exemplified the meaning of this saying. John noted that Jesus did and said many things that were not written down (John 21:25).

We can set a Christian example for others by being good stewards of our own possessions and, therefore, sharing with people in need.

After Paul finished his address, he and the elders knelt in prayer together. A lengthy and emotional farewell followed with the elders embracing and kissing the apostle. This display of emotion with tears and kisses was natural in the culture of that time. Paul's statement that they would not see him again grieved these believers. Finally, they accompanied Paul to the ship.

Paul set an example for others in his character, witness, commitment, and generosity. What kind of Christian example do we set for others?

FOR FURTHER STUDY

1. Read the article "Collection for the Poor Saints" in the *Holman Bible Dictionary*, page 276.

2. Read the article "Miletus" in the *Holman Bible Dictionary*, page 964.

3. See map 121, "The Third Missionary Journey of Paul" in *Holman Bible Atlas*, 249.

4. See the articles "Aristarchus" and "The Third Missionary Journey" in the Winter 2000 issue of *Biblical Illustrator.*

The Week of January 14
STAYING THE COURSE

Background Passage: Acts 21:1-40
Lesson Passages: Acts 21:10-14,27-32

INTRODUCTION

Living in Columbia can prove dangerous because of the powerful influence of the drug cartels in that country. A while back an explosion caused by a drug-related bombing destroyed the nearby home of a Baptist missionary family working in the city of Medellin. The loss of their home forced them to relocate to the capital, Bogota. Despite the fact that they saw and heard glass flying all around them, the missionaries escaped physical harm. In our own country several Christian young people lost their lives in the spring of 1999 in the high school shootings in Littleton, Colorado. The teenage gunmen seemed to target, among others, those who openly professed their faith in the Lord. Believers all around the world sometimes find themselves in difficult, unwanted circumstances simply because they are trying to do what God wants them to do.

This lesson centers on Paul's going to Jerusalem under the Spirit's leadership (Acts 20:22), knowing that he would be bound and delivered over to the Gentiles. The study emphasizes doing God's will even if the consequences seem unreasonable. It challenges us to obey the Lord regardless of the results. Will we accept this challenge and stay the course?

Acts 21:1-40

1. Journey to Jerusalem (21:1-9)
2. Prophetic Warning (21:10-16)
3. Hopeful Strategy (21:17-26)
4. Paul's Arrest (21:27-36)
5. Paul's Plan to Speak (21:37-40)

THE BACKGROUND

After parting from the Ephesian elders at Miletus, Paul continued his voyage to Jerusalem. The narrative of this journey is the third of Luke's four "we" sections in Acts (16:10-17; 20:5-15; 21:1-18; 27:1—28:16). Under the Spirit's leadership, Luke may have based the material in this section on a travel journal kept by himself or one of Paul's companions. It includes various specific details about the trip, such as a detailed listing of the ports and stopping points along the way. It also relates a number of incidents that occurred during the travels.

Many Bible students describe this section as having a journey motif or theme because Luke appears to have been describing Paul's trip to Jerusalem in terms relating to Jesus' going up to Jerusalem to die. Luke knew, of course, that Paul did not die at Jerusalem. Yet he wrote of Paul's journey to the holy city in terms that roughly paralleled that of Jesus' final journey to Jerusalem as told in the Synoptic Gospels. For instance, both Jesus and Paul encountered similar plots by the Jews, a handing over to the Gentiles, a triple prediction on the way of coming suffering (20:22-24; 21:4,10-11; see Luke 9:22,44; 18:32-34), a steadfast obedience, and the same strong resolve to do God's will. Also the companions of both Jesus and Paul had misgivings about continuing to follow the course revealed by the Spirit. In the Gospels Jesus' predictions of His coming passion provide the threatening tone. For Paul's journey, the warnings of Spirit-led Christians along the way served this function. In Jerusalem the authorities arrested Jesus and had Him executed. Years later in Jerusalem the authorities also arrested Paul. Although he did not suffer execution there, he did face extreme danger.

THE LESSON PASSAGE

1. Journey to Jerusalem (Acts 21:1-9)

Luke suggested great emotion in the parting of Paul and his companions from the Ephesian elders with the words "after we had torn ourselves away" (Acts 21:1). He described the journey from Miletus to Tyre in considerable detail, naming each point along the route: Cos, an island off the mainland about 40 miles south of Miletus; the island of Rhodes, whose main city had the same name; and Patara on the Lycian mainland. The group evidently changed at Patara from a coasting to a seagoing vessel in order to make the direct journey to Phoenicia. Paul was still in a hurry to reach Jerusalem. With the limited time available, therefore, he chose a ship that would sail directly across the open sea, a journey of some 400 miles. During this voyage they sighted the island of Cyprus. Passing to the south of it, they sailed on to Syria. Tyre was the main port for merchant traffic between Asia Minor and the holy land, as well as the chief town in Phoenicia, a region in Syria. Paul's ship naturally put in there to unload its cargo.

Evidently the direct open-sea voyage had saved the apostle enough time for him to spend a week with the believers at Tyre and still fulfill his desire to reach Jerusalem by Pentecost. Or perhaps he had to wait a few days while the same ship prepared to sail further or until he found another vessel sailing to Caesarea. Paul and his traveling companions used the time to have fellowship with the Christian community. The Tyrian Christians through the Spirit urged Paul not to go to Jerusalem, foreseeing suffering for him there. Paul, however, possessed a firm conviction that God was leading him to the holy city and had a purpose for him there. The warnings along the way prepared Paul for the imprisonment and hardship he would face, strengthened him for the trying experiences. The warnings also convinced him that God was in all that would come. The Spirit's message enabled Paul's fellow believers to show concern for him.

When the ship was ready to depart, Paul and his companions resumed their journey after an emotion-filled farewell scene. All the Christians of Tyre, with their families, accompanied Paul and his associates to the shore. There they knelt and prayed; then followed long good-byes. Paul's party finally boarded ship, and the Tyrian believers returned home.

The group next stopped at Ptolemais. They spent only a day with the believers of that city, perhaps again being tied to their ship's schedule. Leaving the next day, Paul and his party arrived at Caesarea, the harbor and city built by Herod the Great as the port of Jerusalem and the Roman provincial capital of Judea. There they stayed with Philip, the evangelist. Philip was one of the seven Hellenistic officers appointed in the very early days of the Jerusalem church to supervise the daily distribution of food to those who were in need (6:1-6). Later he engaged in missionary activity in Samaria and in the coastal plain (8:26-40). He had four unmarried daughters who prophesied. The early church recognized women as having the gift of prophecy.

2. Prophetic Warning (Acts 21:10-16)

Verse 10: *After we had been there a number of days, a prophet named Agabus came down from Judea.*

Agabus earlier had come down from Jerusalem to Antioch with some other prophets. At that time Agabus had predicted through the Spirit that a severe famine would spread over the entire Roman world. This occurred in A.D. 46. His words had prompted the collection from the Antioch church to help the poorer believers in Judea (11:27-30). This same prophet *came down* to Caesarea and foretold Paul's arrest and imprisonment. *Agabus,* however, unlike the believers at Tyre who also spoke through the Spirit, did not conclude that Paul should not continue his journey.

Verse 11: *Coming over to us, he took Paul's belt, tied his own hands and feet with it and said, "The Holy Spirit says, 'In this way the Jews of Jerusalem will bind the owner of this belt and will hand him over to the Gentiles.' "*

Agabus predicted Paul's coming arrest in Jerusalem by both an action and words interpreting it. His symbolic act appeared similar to the acted-out prophecies of Old Testament prophets such as Isaiah, who went naked and barefoot for three years to show how the Assyrians would lead the Egyptians into exile (Isa. 20:2-6), and Ezekiel who illustrated the siege of Jerusalem by using clay tablets as models and lying on his side (Ezek. 4:1-17). Agabus *took Paul's belt,* the long cloth wound several times around his waist, and *tied his own hands and feet with it.* Then he interpreted his act, beginning *"The Holy Spirit says."* These words corresponded to "Thus says the Lord" on the lips of Old Testament prophets. Agabus declared that the *Jews of Jerusalem* would *bind* Paul and *hand him over to the Gentiles.*

This saying paralleled Jesus' prediction that He would be delivered into the hands of the Gentiles (see Matt. 20:18-19). The prophecy of Agabus did not have a literal word-for-word fulfillment. Although the Jews did seize Paul, they did not hand him over to the Romans. Instead, the Romans rescued him from the Jewish mob and kept him in custody. The form of Agabus's wording brought out more clearly the parallelism between the fates of Jesus and Paul. In any case, the Jews were responsible for Paul's falling into the hands of the Romans and remaining in prison. Agabus was not trying to urge Paul not to go to Jerusalem; instead, he was telling him what to expect there. Agabus's act and its interpretation prepared Paul for the events to come and assured him of God's presence in those happenings.

Verse 12: *When we heard this, we and the people there pleaded with Paul not to go up to Jerusalem.*

Agabus's dramatic prophecy had a powerful effect. Much like the believers of Tyre, Paul's traveling companions *(we)* and the Caesarean Christians *(the people there)* concluded from this solemn prediction that Paul should not continue his journey. They *pleaded with Paul* with tears (21:13) *not to go up to Jerusalem.* They wanted him to change his plans, but they had no more success than the believers at Tyre.

Verse 13: *Then Paul answered, "Why are you weeping and breaking my heart? I am ready not only to be bound, but also to die in Jerusalem for the name of the Lord Jesus."*

The grief displayed by Paul's friends had the effect of *breaking* his *heart* as they attempted to change his mind. *Breaking* often referred to washing clothes by pounding them with stones. The well-meant pleas of the apostle's friends pounded at him and caused him emotional pain. Paul knew the journey was in God's will for him, and He was willing even *to die* for his Lord if necessary. He would not turn aside from the path of obedience and sacrifice even if it meant giving his life for his Master's sake. This incident showed Paul's complete willingness to do God's will. His determination to go to Jerusalem came from an inward spiritual conviction. He would not dismiss this. It had come to him by the Spirit's direction in response to a growing belief that he must present the gift from the Gentile churches personally in Jerusalem. He wanted others to view the relief offering as the symbol of unity he intended it to be.

Verse 14: *When he would not be dissuaded, we gave up and said, "The Lord's will be done."*

Faced by Paul's determination, his friends finally gave up in their attempt to stop his journey. They did not want to see him suffer. They did not want to lose their leader, but they respected his firm conviction that God wanted him to make this trip to Jerusalem. They prayed that *the Lord's will be done.* These words are similar to those Jesus prayed in the garden of Gethsemane (Luke 22:42). Jesus did not look forward to facing the human agony of the cross, but He committed Himself totally to God's purpose for His life. Many Bible students refer to this event in Acts as Paul's Gethsemane.

Paul and his friends came to the final stage of their journey. They took the road up to Jerusalem, about 65 miles away to the southeast. For this final part of the trip they might have used pack animals. They were carrying the large collection from the Gentile churches. A considerable group made the trip, including Paul, Luke, those delegated by the churches to bear the collection, and some of the Caesarean Christians. The disciples from Caesarea acted as guides in bringing the party to the house of Mnason, a man who was a Christian of long-standing. Since Mnason was a native of Cyprus, he probably belonged to the group of more Hellenistic-minded Jewish Christians from the Dispersion (those living outside the holy land). These people would more likely act as Paul's hosts in Jerusalem than some of the more traditionally minded Jewish believers. Not everyone in the Jerusalem church would have accepted Paul and his company of Gentile converts as house guests during Pentecost. Paul's arrival in Jerusalem completed his third missionary journey.

I remember well the day when I was about to board the plane from North Carolina to Texas to attend Southwestern Baptist Theological Seminary. I did not know anyone in Fort Worth or at the school. As the boarding call sounded, my mother said, "You don't have to go." I did not need to hear those words because of my own fears of leaving home and going to the far-away unknown. Yet I knew God wanted me to go. After a teary farewell hug, I boarded the plane. Well-meaning family and friends sometimes try to deter us from doing what God wants of us. We must stay on His track for our lives.

3. Hopeful Strategy (Acts 21:17-26)

When Paul and his party arrived in Jerusalem, the believers there received them warmly. They probably gathered at Mnason's house. The next day Paul and the rest of the traveling group called on James, the leader of the Jerusalem church. The apostle reported to him and all the elders in detail what God had done among the Gentiles through his ministry. He probably also presented the collection from the Gentile churches to James and the elders, though Luke said nothing about this. Nowhere in Acts (except later in reporting Paul's speech before Felix, 24:17) did Luke mention this collection for the poor Christians at Jerusalem, even though it was the chief purpose of Paul's trip to the holy city.

Paul's audience glorified and praised God for what they heard. Nevertheless, these leaders knew that some people continued to view Paul suspiciously, though they themselves did not share that viewpoint. Paul's success, however, had created some problems for them, so they now described the situation to him. The Jerusalem church was increasingly being caught between its loyalty to the Jewish nation and its support of Paul's Gentile mission. To accept the relief offering from the Gentile believers identified Jewish Christians further with that mission and served as another point of division between themselves and their fellow Jews. Paul arrived in Jerusalem during the rule of Felix, a time of intense Jewish nationalism and political unrest. One rebellion after another rose to challenge the Roman rulers. Felix cruelly suppressed them all. His actions increased the Jewish hatred for Rome and stirred up anti-Gentile sentiments.

With the growing tide of Jewish nationalism, Jewish Christians found more and more difficulty in supporting the Gentile mission. The Jerusalem church with its thousands of Jewish converts wanted to maintain its relations with the nation and keep open opportunities for further outreach to Israel. The church leaders did not want to reject Paul, yet they had their own mission to the Jews to consider. The situation called for wisdom, understanding, and diplomacy.

Those "zealous for the law" (v. 20) believed the false rumors about Paul circulating among the Jewish Christians of Jerusalem. These rumors contended that the apostle not only refused to impose the requirement of the Jewish law on his Gentile converts, but also he actually advised Jews who lived in Gentile communities to forsake the law of Moses, to abandon the practice of circumcising their children, and to turn away from the customs laid down in the law—in other words, to abandon their Jewish heritage. These matters struck at the very heart of the Jews' self-identity as the people of God, making the charges serious. Even though Paul proclaimed that Christ was the end of the law, no evidence exists that he actively persuaded Jewish Christians to abandon circumcising their children or to give up Jewish customs. Paul himself had Timothy circumcised (16:3) and personally undertook a Nazirite vow (18:18). For Paul, being in Christ did not require that the Gentile become a Jew or that the Jew stop being a Jew. James and the elders apparently regarded these rumors as false. They knew, however, that Paul had to convince the many zealots in the Jerusalem church of the truth about the apostle and his teachings.

The leaders of the church suggested something practical that Paul could do to make clear to everyone that he was still true to the Jewish law. He could publicly take part in one of the ancestral customs, proving that he was, after all, a pious and obedient Jew. Therefore, they urged Paul to join with four Jewish Christians who were fulfilling their Nazirite vows, an extreme expression of Jewish piety. The four were nearing the end of the period of their vows. They would soon be completing it with the customary ceremony in the temple. This involved cutting their hair and burning it as an offering. The law also required a number of costly sacrifices. The elders asked the apostle to bear the expense of these rites. To pay the charges for the Nazirite offerings represented an accepted act of Jewish piety and identified one with the Jewish people. This would show Paul's loyalty to the law, not only in his bearing the heavy expenses of the vow but also in his undergoing the purification necessary to participate in the concluding temple ceremony.

While the church leaders asked Paul to behave in this way, they did not make demands of the Gentile believers. James assured Paul that they had not changed the basic decision of the Jerusalem Conference (Acts 15). Gentiles still enjoyed freedom from living by the Jewish law. They only were asked to observe those basic ritual matters that made table fellowship and social interaction possible between Jewish and Gentile Christians. The church council had given four injunctions (21:25) for the sake of harmony within the church and not to hinder the progress of the Jewish Christian mission.

Paul accepted the request. He possessed a willingness to become all things to all people for the gospel's sake, including becoming a Jew to the Jews (1 Cor. 9:19-23). His participation in this symbolic act of Jewish piety would help justify his Gentile mission in the eyes of Jewish Christians. Coming from Gentile lands, Paul would have had to regain ceremonial purity by a seven-day purification ritual before he could qualify for participation in the completion ceremony in the temple for the four Jewish Christians. This ritual included reporting to one of the priests and being sprinkled with water of atonement on the third and seventh days.

On the day following his meeting with James and the elders, the apostle went to the temple to begin his own period of cleansing from ritual defilement. He also informed the priests that he was providing the funds for the offerings of the four men who had taken Nazirite vows and announced the date that they would conclude these vows and when he would complete his own purification.

4. Paul's Arrest (Acts 21:27-36)

Verse 27: *When the seven days were nearly over, some Jews from the province of Asia saw Paul at the temple. They stirred up the whole crowd and seized him,*

Paul's purification process required a cleansing on the third and seventh days. As he returned to the temple toward the end of his seven-day purification (possibly when he came to receive the water of atonement on the seventh day), the trouble began. The strict Jewish Christians from Jerusalem with whom he was attempting to reconcile did not cause the trouble, but Jews from the Roman province of *Asia* in western Asia Minor did. They probably were from Ephesus, and they **stirred up the whole crowd** against Paul and **seized him.**

Paul had spent three years in Ephesus and part of the time in the synagogue. The Jews there knew him well. In his Miletus address Paul had referred to plots the Ephesian Jews already had directed against him. Often Jews who lived outside the holy land were strict in their observance of the Jewish ritual. They did not want to conform to the pagans around them. These Asian Jews almost certainly had come to Jerusalem as pilgrims for the festival of Pentecost. They might have spread false rumors about Paul throughout Jerusalem. When they found Paul at the temple, they determined to take more effective measures against him than had been possible in Ephesus.

Verse 28: *shouting, "Men of Israel, help us! This is the man who teaches all men everywhere against our people and our law and this place. And besides, he has brought Greeks into the temple area and defiled this holy place."*

The Asian Jews shouted out serious accusations against Paul to the **men of Israel** in the temple courts. They accused Paul of teaching against **our people and our law and this place,** the temple. Earlier in the church's history the Jews had made the latter two charges also against Stephen (6:13). The third charge, though less specific, had perhaps the most validity—that Paul had taught against *our people.* The apostle taught the gospel of the oneness of all in Jesus Christ, Greek as well as Jew. This ultimately reduced the significance of the Jews as God's chosen people.

The Asian Jews also accused Paul of having violated the temple by bringing **Greeks** or Gentiles beyond the court of the Gentiles into the sacred courts open only to Jews. They claimed Paul thus had **defiled this holy place.** The temple in Jerusalem had several concentric rectangular courts. Gentiles could enter the outermost court, called the court of the Gentiles. They could not enter the temple proper. In fact, a stone barrier separated the court of the Gentiles from the first courtyard of the temple proper, the court of the women. This low barrier had warning stones set at regular intervals, some with warnings written in Greek and some in Latin. These forbade foreigners or non-Jews access beyond that point. Any foreigner proceeding beyond the barrier did so on pain of death. Roman authorities were so conciliatory of Jewish ideas about this matter that they ratified the death penalty for any Gentile—even a Roman citizen—caught going beyond that wall. The Jewish ideas about temple purity contained such emotion that the charge made against Paul led to a riot.

Verse 29: *(They had previously seen Trophimus the Ephesian in the city with Paul and assumed that Paul had brought him into the temple area.)*

Acts makes clear that the charge the Asian Jews made against Paul was false. Luke explained that they had seen Paul with the Gentile ***Trophimus the Ephesian in the city.*** This man represented the Asian churches in the collection delegation. The Ephesian Jews had recognized Trophimus as one of their own fellow citizens. They assumed Trophimus had accompanied Paul into the inner courts of the temple. Paul had gone into the inner area of the temple in connection with his purification rites, but he had not taken Trophimus there. On an occasion when he was trying to establish his identity with the Jews, he would have done nothing to jeopardize that relationship. The Jews ironically accused the apostle of having defiled the temple at the same time he was there for his own purification.

Verse 30: *The whole city was aroused, and the people came running from all directions. Seizing Paul, they dragged him from the temple, and immediately the gates were shut.*

The uproar quickly spread; the ***whole city was aroused.*** The temple area served somewhat as a town square. The court of the Gentiles covered a large area and enabled large crowds to gather there. When the shouting started, ***people came running from all directions.*** They seized Paul in one of the inner courts of the temple and ***dragged him*** out to the court of the Gentiles. Then the temple police who patrolled the area and stood guard at the gates leading into the inner courts closed the gates leading from the outer into the inner courts. This prevented the inner courts from being defiled by the mob action taking place and possible bloodshed.

Verse 31: *While they were trying to kill him, news reached the commander of the Roman troops that the whole city of Jerusalem was in an uproar.*

Quickly news of the disturbance reached the ***commander of the Roman troops*** garrisoned in the Fortress of Antonia. This complex stood northwest of the temple precincts. Herod the Great had built the fortress for defense of the temple. The fortress overlooked the temple area to the south and the city to the north and west with stair exits connecting it to both the court of the Gentiles and the city proper. The Romans realized that should any unrest occur in the city, it probably would begin in the temple area. Antonia had several high towers, at least one of which allowed a full view of the entire temple area. Perhaps a sentry on duty there caught sight of the gathering mob and sent word to his commander, the Roman officer in charge of the Jerusalem troops.

While some of the Levites served as the temple police, the commander of the fortress was a Roman military officer. He had the responsibility of keeping peace in the city. Luke later gave the name of this man, Claudius Lysias (23:26). This tribune, a high-ranking Roman military officer, had charge of a cohort. A cohort normally consisted of 1,000 soldiers (760 infantry and 240 cavalry). Since the procurator resided in Caesarea and only made periodic visits to Jerusalem, this commander had the main responsibility for the Roman administration and peace-keeping of the city.

Verse 32: *He at once took some officers and soldiers and ran down to the crowd. When the rioters saw the commander and his soldiers, they stopped beating Paul.*

The commander acted *at once* to deal with the riot by taking *some officers* (centurions) *and soldiers* down into the temple crowd. Since a centurion commanded a hundred soldiers and since Luke indicated more than one centurion, Lysias's force could have numbered up to 200. The appearance of this strong Roman force made the crowd fall back and stop *beating* Paul. The Roman intervention probably saved Paul's life. Since the apostle appeared to be the cause of the unrest, Lysias immediately arrested him and bound him with two chains.

Undoubtedly *the commander* thought Paul was a criminal and treated him as one. When Lysias asked the mob about his crime, however, he got no clear answer because of the mob disorder. As with most mobs, many of the people probably did not know what the confusion was all about. So Lysias ordered the soldiers to take Paul to the quiet of the barracks where he could conduct a more orderly examination of the prisoner and his accusers. The crowd, however, renewed their rioting and made it impossible for Paul to walk in safety up the stairway to the fortress. The soldiers had to lift him up and carry him to protect him from the violence of the mob. As they hurried up the steps, the crowd followed shouting "Away with him!" (21:36). They had screamed these same words against Jesus. Basically, they meant *Kill him!*

Paul was committed to following God's leadership and fulfilling His purposes for him, no matter what the cost. We also can commit ourselves to follow God's leadership regardless of the consequences. People may misunderstand us or even violently oppose us when we seek to do what God wants us to do. Obedience to the Lord may or may not bring difficulties. In either case, that should not stop us. We should stay on God's course for our lives. He promises us the comfort of His presence, gives us His strength, and assures us of the ultimate victory.

5. Paul's Plan to Speak (Acts 21:37-40)

At the top of the stone stairway leading into the Fortress of Antonia Paul requested permission to say something to Claudius Lysias. The commander was amazed to hear his prisoner speaking in fluent Greek. He had suspected Paul of being an uneducated revolutionary, perhaps the Egyptian who had led a large band of followers into the wilderness some time before. He described the Egyptian's followers as terrorists. Felix and his soldiers had driven him off.

Paul's reply revealed that he wanted to establish his respectable Jewish background and civil status. He was not a terrorist or the kind of person to cause a riot in the temple. He was a Jew and a citizen of Tarsus. He had great pride in his citizenship in this self-governing city. His own Jewish background gave him some basis for addressing his fellow Jews. His obvious culture and education assured Lysias that he was not one of the rabble and deserved to have his request honored. With the assurance of Paul's credentials, Lysias allowed him to address the crowd.

The apostle stood at the top of the steps, brought a hush over the crowd with a wave of his hand, and addressed them in Aramaic, their own native tongue. Paul gave a speech to defend himself against the charges that he had taught against the Jewish people, the law, and the temple.

FOR FURTHER STUDY
1. Read "The Temple in Jesus' Day" in the Summer 1988 issue of *Biblical Illustrator.*
2. Read "The Fortress Antonia" in the Spring 1989 issue of *Biblical Illustrator.*
3. Read about the Nazirite vow in Numbers 6:1-21.
4. See the articles "Caesarea by the Sea" and "The Third Missionary Journey" in the Winter 2000 issue of *Biblical Illustrator.*

The Week of January 21
VALUING HUMAN LIFE

Background Passages: Genesis 1:27; Matthew 5:13-16,21-22,27-28,
43-45a
Lesson Passages: Genesis 1:27; Matthew 5:13-16, 21-22, 27-28, 43-45a

INTRODUCTION

In August 1999, as Hurricane Bret moved toward the Texas Gulf coast, authorities encouraged residents in the area targeted for landfall to evacuate. Thousands did. In that same month a powerful earthquake devastated parts of Turkey. Rescuers worked for hours to free people trapped beneath layers of collapsed buildings. These two incidents show that many people place a high value on human life.

Yet at the same time these incidents occurred, television news reported the arrest of a convicted child molester in the kidnapping of a six-year-old girl. The newspaper arrived at our door with stories of murder, assault, and drug abuse. During that same time I also read in an evangelical magazine how an African government appeared to be withholding food in order to starve into submission thousands of refugees forced from their tribal homelands. These events show that many around us do not value human life. In fact, they seem intent on destroying it.

On this week of Sanctity of Human Life Sunday, this study emphasizes the high value that our Creator places on human life and the value that we in turn should place on every human being.

Genesis 1:27; Matthew 5:13-16,21-22,27-28,43-45a

1. In God's Image (Gen. 1:27)
2. Salt and Light (Matt. 5:13-16)
3. Murder and Anger (Matt. 5:21-22)
4. Adultery (Matt. 5:27-28)
5. Love for Enemies (Matt. 5:43-45a)

THE BACKGROUND

Sanctity means the quality of being considered sacred. The phrase *sanctity of human life* points to the value of human beings. Each individual deserves respect. Why?

The lesson passages provide biblical principles to answer that question. The focus on the sanctity of life begins with the Creator of life (Gen. 1). God's creative act in making men and women in His image is the foundation for understanding why each individual life is sacred.

The remaining four passages of the lesson come from the first chapter of the Sermon on the Mount (Matt. 5—7). These passages present the character, duties, attitudes, and dangers of the Christian disciple. It shows how those who belong to Christ are to think and to act.

The lesson verses from Matthew 5 present principles that relate to the sanctity of human life. Believers should live in ways that show their relationship to Jesus Christ (5:13-16). Instead of withdrawing from society, they should influence the world around them. This includes valuing human life, recognizing that hatred for others shows disrespect for life (5:21-22). Upholding purity in sexual relationships shows respect for others and obedience to God's laws (5:27-28). Finally, Jesus' command to love others, including one's enemies, indicates the high value Jesus wants us to place on all people (5:43-45a).

THE LESSON PASSAGE

1. In God's Image (Gen. 1:27)

Verse 27: *So God created man in his own image,*
in the image of God he created him;
male and female he created them.

As the crowning event of creation week, **God created** humankind. The Hebrew word for **man** used here, *adam,* is the generic term for *man* or humanity. It thus includes woman. Although humanity shared creation day with the larger animals and has some relationship to them, humankind possesses a uniqueness and importance the animals lack. The Bible portrays men and women as special creatures, set apart from the rest of God's works. Genesis 1:27 states three times that *God created* humans, using the Hebrew verb *bara*, which indicates a special creation.

As His special creation, God made human beings in His own "image" and "likeness" (1:26). The word *image* indicates representative figure. It describes an exact resemblance, like a son who is the very image of his father. "Likeness" or appearance seems to emphasize that though people are like God, they are not God. Men and women are not deity but reflect the divine nature within their humanity. This image of God characterizes all humans but not the animals.

The *image of God* does not refer to the physical bodily form of human life. Rather, it probably refers to those qualities of humanity that are like God. These could include a high capacity for intelligence and reason, a personality with the power of self-consciousness and self-determination, and the abilities to act as moral creatures within God's standards of right and wrong, to make choices, to make commitments, and to have personal relationships. Because God created people in His image, they can enjoy a fellowship with Him not possible for other creatures. No other created beings have the capacity for fellowship with their Creator as do humans.

God also created humans as **male and female.** God's creation of humanity included a sexual distinction, but woman and man both share equally in God's image. To define humanity as bisexual makes each partner the complement of the other and anticipates the New Testament doctrine of the spiritual equality of men and women (Gal. 3:28). This does not negate the leadership-followship roles of Genesis 2 and Ephesians 5:22-33, however.

God commanded people not only to reproduce and populate the earth but also to establish control over the earth and its resources ("subdue it," Gen. 1:28). Basically, God gave them dominion over all that He had previously created. God created people to have a superior position within but at the head of all creation. Though a special creation, they always remain under the supreme authority of God.

God is the source of life. He created people with conscience, dignity, and the ability to have fellowship with Him. His image in us requires that we take all human beings seriously. We dare not treat lightly or harm those created by God. We can show gratitude to God for giving us life by working to oppose destructive behavior that threatens and cheapens others, such as drug abuse, child and spouse abuse, and abortion. We can work to promote alternatives to such behavior, such as supporting counseling programs or volunteering at crisis pregnancy centers. We can also share generously of our resources to help needy people who barely have the basics to sustain life.

2. Salt and Light (Matt. 5:13-16)

The Sermon on the Mount contains principles that support the sanctity of human life. Believers can promote a quality of life for all people by using their influence in each setting where God places them.

Verse 13: *You are the salt of the earth. But if the salt loses its saltiness, how can it be made salty again? It is no longer good for anything, except to be thrown out and trampled by men.*

Jesus described His followers as the **salt of the earth.** He knew that believers have great importance for the unbelieving world. *Salt* had many uses in biblical times, but it functioned mainly as a preservative for food.

Jesus wanted His disciples to help stop corruption and moral decay in their society. Christians are to take a stand against all that deprives people of dignity, respect, health, and justice. They are to promote the well-being of all people, not simply to feather their own nests.

Though people in Jesus' day used salt primarily to preserve food, did Jesus have other possible functions in mind? For instance, salt as a spice flavors food and makes its taste more appealing. Yet in the first century the amount of salt needed to preserve meat without refrigeration meant ancient Jews probably did not consider salt primarily as enhancing taste. Nevertheless, believers can "spice up" life by bringing a special kind of grace and joy to a world that otherwise is often ugly and unhappy.

Jesus spoke of salt that *loses its saltiness.* Strictly speaking, pure salt cannot lose its saltiness since sodium chloride is a stable compound. However, the salt to which Jesus referred came from the Dead Sea area. It was salt mixed with other minerals, such as calcium. Excessive moisture could dissolve and wash away the sodium chloride. Consequently, the "salt" could become worthless as a preservative.

To be thrown out and trampled by men does not refer to eternal security. Rather, it refers to Christians who do not function as they should. Believers whose character and behavior do not reflect kingdom values have no use as agents of change and redemption. When they simply try to fit in and live as the people around them do rather than try to make a difference for good, they are good for nothing.

Verse 14: *You are the light of the world. A city on a hill cannot be hidden.*

Jesus also described His followers as the **light of the world.** *Light* typically serves as a religious symbol. In both Old and New Testaments it most frequently symbolizes purity as opposed to filth, truth as opposed to error, knowledge as opposed to ignorance, and divine revelation and presence as opposed to moral lostness and abandonment by God. Consequently, believers as the *light of the world* should function actively in dispelling darkness in any form whether it relates to impurity, error, ignorance, immorality, or separation from God. They can bring a divine perspective to the affairs of individuals and society. They can show the way to God, the God who cares about all people.

The light that Christians reflect does not come from themselves but derives from Christ, who is Himself the Light of the World (John 8:12; 9:5). Believers have the opportunity to show others how they too can walk in the light and not remain in darkness. Light, like salt, affects its surroundings by being distinct. Disciples who visibly differ from other people in positive ways will have an effect on them.

The image of a *city on a hill* stresses the importance of believers being noticeably different. Often built of white limestone, an ancient city on an elevated area gleamed in the sun and could not *be hidden.* Those who follow Christ should lead lives that sparkle and shine, drawing the attention of all who cross their paths to Christ who transforms lives.

Verse 15: *Neither do people light a lamp and put it under a bowl. Instead they put it on its stand, and it gives light to everyone in the house.*

As a city on a hill cannot be hidden, so also believers should not hide their lights. No one ever would *light a lamp and put it under a bowl.* Instead people put a lamp on a lampstand to give *light to everyone in the house.* Jesus referred to a small lamp that could be held in the palm of the hand. It was fueled by olive oil.

Jesus probably had in mind bringing spiritual light through the revelation of God's salvation. Believers who conceal their faith from others hide the light. They have no more use in the world than those who have lost their saltiness, that is, their distinctiveness. Believers' lives should reflect Jesus, the Light of the world, so others might know Him.

Verse 16: *In the same way, let your light shine before men, that they may see your good deeds and praise your Father in heaven.*

As a lamp inside a house provides light for all within it, Christians are to let their *light shine before* others so others *may see* their *good deeds and praise* their *Father in heaven. Good deeds* include everything Christians do and say that reflects the mind and will of God. Witness includes deeds as well as words, especially actions that protect people and meet their needs. Jesus wants others to see these good works of His disciples. Bringing honor and praise to God, the source of all light, should motivate believers to let their light shine in witness and acts of loving service. Christians should not seek to glorify themselves or parade their own virtue. They should direct attention to the God who transformed them and made them to become lights of the world.

Later in the Sermon on the Mount Jesus warned His followers about practicing acts of righteousness before others "to be seen by them" (6:1). That does not contradict His command for believers to let their light shine before others. In chapter 6 Jesus spoke of glorifying self as the motive for good behavior rather than bringing glory to God.

Our lives should demonstrate our relationship to Jesus Christ. The images of salt and light imply that we believers should not withdraw from society. We must remain active in our roles as salt and light in calling the world to follow God. As salt, we hinder decay and warn others of the dangers of compromise and conformity to the world. As light, we illumine a sin-darkened world and show the way to God.

3. Murder and Anger (Matt. 5:21-22)

Jesus did not come to contradict the law but to fulfill it, to bring the law to its intended goal (5:17). He gave six examples, contrasting what the law said and its traditional interpretation with His stricter requirements. Christ demanded a higher righteousness of His disciples. The six illustrations include His teachings on murder (5:21-26), adultery (5:27-30), divorce (5:31-32), oaths (5:33-37), retaliation (5:38-42), and loving enemies (5:43-38). All of these teachings assume the sanctity of human life and stress the importance of relating to others in ways that honor them as people precious to God.

Verse 21: *You have heard that it was said to the people long ago, 'Do not murder, and anyone who murders will be subject to judgment.'*

Jesus repeated what was spoken **to the people long ago** or in ancient times. He was referring to the Sixth Commandment of the Ten Commandments given on Mount Sinai (Ex. 20:13; Deut. 5:17): **Do not murder.** Jesus' contemporaries understood this law against murder and agreed that a murderer must be brought to judgment. His listeners gained their knowledge of the law by hearing it read in the synagogues.

The word translated *murder* comes from a root word meaning to dash in pieces. It was used to mean kill in a general sense or to mean murder. The Hebrews understood it to mean *do not murder* (and the Old Testament context supports this). In other words, this law did not include killing in self-defense, wars ordered by the Lord, capital punishment following due process of law, or accidental manslaughter. The clause **anyone who murders will be subject to judgment** expands the prohibition of murder found in the Sixth Commandment. *Subject to* means liable. These words summarized the Old Testament teaching on the penalty for murder. In the light of the Old Testament background, this probably referred to judgment by a human court. Jesus, however, in His next words went beyond this to the divine judgment.

Verse 22: *But I tell you that anyone who is angry with his brother will be subject to judgment. Again anyone who says to his brother, 'Raca,' is answerable to the Sanhedrin. But anyone who says, 'You fool!' will be in danger of the fire of hell.*

Jesus showed that murder has its roots in a heart filled with anger and contempt. The words **but I tell you** do not indicate that Jesus was criticizing the Old Testament. Instead He tried to correct the incomplete understanding of the Commandment that many of His hearers had adopted. He spoke on His own authority as the One who fulfilled or established the law (5:17). *I tell you* marked Jesus' authority as Lawgiver and Judge.

Like Moses, Jesus condemned murder; but He also pointed out that harboring **anger** in one's heart is wrong and deserves punishment. Anger and hatred t make one guilty in the sight of God. Jesus assumed the continued validity of the Sixth Commandment, but He rejected a legalistic interpretation that restricted its application to the literal act. One has not conformed to the higher righteousness of God's kingdom simply by refraining from murder. God Himself will bring the angry person to judgment.

Brother in Matthew's Gospel, when not referring to a male sibling, usually refers to Jesus' disciples. Jesus was not implying, however, that His followers had the right to be angry against nonbelievers. He was applying His command first of all to those against whom anger is most inappropriate. Christians should get rid of anger against one another.

Some later New Testament manuscripts added the phrase "without a cause" following the word **brother.** This phrase does not appear in the manuscripts textual scholars consider most reliable. These words, nevertheless, give the correct interpretation. Anger certainly has the restriction of "without a cause." One can have righteous indignation without sinning. Jesus expressed anger on a number of occasions. He drove out all who were buying and selling in the temple (21:12-13). He voiced His anger at the hypocrisy of the Pharisees, calling them blind fools (23:17). The hard hearts of rigid, uncaring legalists angered and disturbed Him (Mark 3:1-5). Jesus' anger, however, came not out of a personal wounded pride but from outrage at injustice, sin, unbelief, and the exploitation of others. Those are legitimate causes for anger, and such anger should motivate us to correct abuses, not to insult or harm the abusers.

Harboring anger over personal pain caused us by others is not justified. Personal slights or insults seem to anger Jesus' followers today more often than moral outrage. Too often that anger leads to vengeful and destructive behavior rather than to forgiveness and actions toward reconciliation.

Jesus further illustrated His teaching that not just murder but also anger is sinful. He used three parallel statements to make the same point in different ways; Jesus was not dealing with three different sins. The first part of each statement indicates the attitude Jesus condemned, and the second relates to its penalty. Anger against a brother expressed itself in insulting language such as **raca.** *Raca* was an Aramaic term of abuse. Perhaps it meant brainless or empty-headed. It definitely expressed contempt.

Those who say to someone ***you fool*** also commit a sin. *Fool* carries the idea of immorality and godlessness as well as idiocy. Jesus Himself used the term *fool* to condemn the hypocrisy of the teachers of the law (Matt. 23:17). (A close reading of Matt. 23:13-39 will show that Jesus' harsh words were intended as a redemptive warning.) Jesus was referring in Matthew 5:22 to violent passion that resulted in fierce name-calling. This behavior is indicative of a person's acting from anger with a motivation of causing harm to one who has caused that person harm. This kind of action makes a person liable to judgment.

Some Bible students give weight to the increasing severity of judgment as Jesus progressed from the term *judgment* to the **Sanhedrin** (the Jewish supreme court) to the ***fire of hell.*** The expression *fire of hell* comes from the Hebrew *Gehenna.* This referred to the Valley of Hinnom, a valley south of Jerusalem once associated with the cult of the pagan god Molech and its terrible rites of child sacrifice, a practice God clearly had prohibited (Deut. 18:10). When King Josiah abolished the practice, he defiled this valley by making it a dumping ground for filth and the corpses of criminals (2 Kings 23:10-14). Apparently first-century people still used the place as a garbage dump, complete with smoldering fires. Jesus and Jewish writers regularly used the term for the place of eternal judgment.

Rather than intending His hearers to take the three terms—judgment, Sanhedrin, fire of hell—as progressive, Jesus most likely intended them to see the terms simply as indicating the seriousness of harboring anger against one another. If Jesus' words were meant to suggest a growing climax of punishments, we would expect a similar increase in the types of offenses. Yet no clear distinction exists among the person with seething anger, the one who prefers Raca as his term of abuse, and the one who insultingly calls his brother a fool. Consequently, all three penalties refer to the danger of facing God's judgment. In contrast with the human court's verdict on murder, Jesus warned about ultimate divine judgment on anger, even that expressed in everyday insults as well as in murder. Jesus wanted His followers to submit their attitudes, words, and actions toward other people to God's careful inspection.

Anger threatens the value of life by undermining the self-esteem of others. It leads to broken relationships. We can enhance the quality of our lives and the lives of others by controlling our anger with God's help.

4. Adultery (Matt. 5:27-28)

Verse 27: *"You have heard that it was said, 'Do not commit adultery.'*
Jesus turned from the Sixth to the Seventh Commandment (Ex. 20:14): **do not commit adultery.** *Adultery* usually referred to sexual relations by a married person with a partner other than that person's spouse. Jewish sources often treated this command as if it related to theft, not purity. For them, adultery meant stealing another's spouse.

Verse 28: *But I tell you that anyone who looks at a woman lustfully has already committed adultery with her in his heart.*
Jesus stressed the spirit of the Commandment and did not limit it to married people. He was referring to sexual sin in general. Once more Jesus spoke with His own authority—**but I tell you.** Again, He focused on the inward thoughts or attitudes that lead to outward acts. In this case misplaced desire in the heart leads to outward sexual sin. The grammar of this verse permits two possible translations. Jesus could have spoken of one who looks at a woman with the intention of committing adultery, or His words could refer to one who looks at a woman for the purpose of getting her to lust after him. The force of the verb tense translated **looks** means continuing to look rather than merely casting a passing glance. **Lustfully** literally means in order to desire her. The word referred typically to the desire for something forbidden.

To some extent, attraction between men and women is natural. Jesus was not condemning that. He was, however, clearly condemning the cultivation of a desire for an illicit relationship. He meant lustful thoughts—those that focused on an actual desire to have sexual relations with one other than one's spouse. The command's intent applies equally to men and to women. Anyone, either married or unmarried, who continues to look at another with a persistent lust to have sex with that person *has already committed adultery* with him or her in the heart. The tense of *committed* indicates an act occurring at a point in time in the past. The sin already has been committed in the heart. This makes it a sin as is the real, physical act. Jesus' strict interpretation of the Seventh Commandment did not cancel the law as stated but explained it in terms of its true meaning.

We are to value others as people of worth, not as objects of sexual desire. We should recognize adultery as destructive behavior that affects many people beyond the couple committing the act. Are there habits we need to change in our lives to strengthen the purity of our own thoughts and the way we look at others? For instance, we may have to stop watching some television programs, refuse to go to some movies, and select our reading material more carefully. We may have to guard our thoughts in the presence of people we find interesting or attractive. God will help us to find the way of escape when temptation comes.

5. Love for Enemies (Matt. 5:43-45a)

Verse 43: *You have heard that it was said, 'Love your neighbor and hate your enemy.'*

Once more Jesus quoted from the Old Testament and added a popular saying as well. *Love your neighbor* comes from Leviticus 19:18, but *hate your enemies* appears nowhere in the Old Testament. Some Bible students believe the Hebrews drew this latter saying from texts such as Deuteronomy 23:3-6 (not allowing Ammonites or Moabites into the assembly or seeking peace with them) or Psalm 139:21 (hating those who hate the Lord). The Qumran community, a Jewish sect present in the first century A.D., had a manual that explicitly commanded love for those within its fellowship. Other groups probably held similar positions. Jesus' words attacked the popular attitude these groups shared and perhaps intensified. Whatever the source, hatred of enemies was common enough in Jesus' day to fit under the category of something Jesus' audience had heard *that it was said.*

Verse 44: *But I tell you: Love your enemies and pray for those who persecute you,*

Again Jesus returned to the true spirit of the Old Testament, which commanded compassion for aliens in the community (Ex. 22:21). Also the story of Ruth showed that the Hebrews did embrace some Moabites. She became an ancestor of the Messiah. Jesus outlined a more demanding ethic: *love your enemies.* The term *enemies* in this context may primarily represent those opposed to God's people, though it need not be limited to that application. Some may oppose us out of jealousy or competition.

The disciples' attitude toward *those who persecute* them must go beyond revenge to a positive love. The love of those who follow Jesus should exclude no one. Jesus desired a universal love that shows no discrimination. He referred not to mere affection but to *agape* love—generous, warm, costly self-sacrifice for another's good. Love for enemies will result in prayer for them. Praying for enemies and loving them will prove mutually reinforcing. The more believers love, the more they will pray. The more they pray, the more they will love.

Verse 45a: *that you may be sons of your Father in heaven.*

Love for enemies identifies disciples as **sons** of their **Father,** for children share their father's character. God's love includes everyone (John 3:16). Our Father's example provides the motivation for Jesus' disciples to act like their Father. Indeed, how believers treat those who hate or who mistreat them is a test of the genuineness of Christian faith. We show that we value human life by treating all people, even enemies, with a love that is warm, generous, and self-sacrificial.

As wrong as abortion is as a violation of the sanctity of human life, believers must use lawful actions to oppose the legal system and those who perform abortions, not actions marked by violence and hate. In all Christians do they are to show their relationship to Jesus Christ. When Christians march with posters describing homosexuals with ugly names, they do not show that they are children of God. Jesus commands His people to love and to pray for all people. By so doing, they demonstrate obedience to Him and acknowledge the sanctity of all human life.

FOR FURTHER STUDY

1. Read "Lamps in Ancient Israel" in the Winter 1996 issue of *Biblical Illustrator.*

2. See "The Meaning of 'Raca'" in the Winter 1996 issue of *Biblical Illustrator.*

3. Read "The Laws behind Jesus' Teaching" in the Winter 1996 issue of *Biblical Illustrator.*

4. See the article "Sermon on the Mount" in the *Holman Bible Dictionary,* 1247-1248.

The Week of January 28

SHARING YOUR TESTIMONY

Background Passage: Acts 22:1—23:35
Lesson Passages: Acts 22:3-4,6-13,16-21

INTRODUCTION

All of us who have come to know Jesus Christ as our personal Lord and Savior have some good news to share. Some years ago while participating in evangelism training, I had to write out my personal testimony. The director of the witnessing training gave me and the other participants a three-point model to follow in developing our testimonies—my life before Christ, how I became a Christian, and how Christ changed my life.

This lesson examines Paul's defense before the Jews who had attacked him and provides the basis for the model testimony we used in our training. This lesson challenges us to use Paul's model to share our testimonies with others.

Acts 22:1—23:35

1. Paul's Testimony to the Jews (22:1-22)
2. Paul Identified as a Roman Citizen (22:23-29)
3. Paul Before the Sanhedrin (22:30—23:11)
4. Plot to Kill Paul (23:12-22)
5. Paul Sent to Caesarea (23:23-35)

THE BACKGROUND

Paul returned to Jerusalem at the end of his third missionary journey. He carried with him the relief offering he had collected from the Gentile churches. Delegates from these churches accompanied the apostle and shared in the presentation of this gift. Paul participated in the completion ceremony of four Jewish believers who had taken a Nazirite vow. Jews from Ephesus saw Paul in the temple and falsely accused him of taking a Gentile into the area designated for Jews only. The resulting riot threatened Paul's life. Roman soldiers rescued him from the mob. Paul asked for and received permission to speak to the crowd.

Paul's arrest, his request to address the people, and his defense speech begin the lengthy account of his imprisonment and trials in Jerusalem and Caesarea as well as his journey to Rome to to be tried there. One fourth of Acts is devoted to this period that includes several court appearances by Paul, three of Paul's lengthy speeches, and two repetitions of the story of his conversion. Paul is seen not only as a missionary and church planter but also as a witness on trial for the gospel. The first of Paul's five defenses (22:1-21) highlights the nonpolitical character of Christianity and presents the apostle's mission to the Gentiles as the major reason for Jewish opposition to the gospel.

THE LESSON PASSAGE

1. Paul's Testimony to the Jews (Acts 22:1-22) ‹

Paul wanted to speak to the temple crowd to prove his full commitment to Judaism. Paul's conversion account being included three times in Acts emphasizes the event and shows its importance. In his testimonies, the apostle stressed details that would best fit his audience and purpose. For instance, when speaking to the Jewish crowd, Paul told about Ananias and his reputation as a devout Jew. In the later speech before Agrippa and the Roman officials he did not mention Ananias (26:1-29).

Paul used formal Jewish terms of address, "Brothers and fathers" (22:1). These respectful titles were designed to help his hearers identify with him. The apostle described his speech in formal language as a "defense." By that term, Paul meant more than answering charges made in court; he also included the idea of witness. Paul used the opportunity to testify about Jesus Christ. Actually, he did not even address the charge that had started the riot—that he had defiled the temple. Instead, he chose to address the larger issue—his faithfulness to Judaism. The crowd became more attentive as the apostle began to speak in Aramaic. Using their own language further emphasized Paul's Jewishness.

Verse 3: *"I am a Jew, born in Tarsus of Cilicia, but brought up in this city. Under Gamaliel I was thoroughly trained in the law of our fathers and was just as zealous for God as any of you are today.*

Paul began by affirming himself as a loyal **Jew.** He was **born in Tarsus of Cilicia,** but his upbringing took place in **this city,** Jerusalem. Evidently Paul's family must have moved to Jerusalem at a very early stage in his life. The apostle wanted this crowd to know of his nurture in the holy city. Despite leaving Tarsus at an early age, Paul must have maintained family contacts with his hometown. He had returned to Tarsus as a missionary early in his Christian life (9:30).

Paul had studied in Jerusalem **under Gamaliel,** a leading Pharisee teacher. Thus he had been **thoroughly trained in the law of our fathers.** Paul's birth, upbringing, and education reflected a common biographical formula common in Greek writings to describe a man's youth. Paul used these three facts to establish his Jewishness. Far from being a lawbreak-er, Paul's former life showed him as *zealous for God as any* of those in the crowd before him.

Verse 4: *I persecuted the followers of this Way to their death, arresting both men and women and throwing them into prison,*

As evidence of his zeal for God and the Jewish religion, Paul described his former days as a persecutor of the **followers of this Way** (Christianity) in Jerusalem and elsewhere (9:2). Jesus identified Himself as the *Way* (John 14:6). To persecute the Way was to persecute Christ Himself. Paul had gone further than his audience in religious zeal. He had arrested **both men and women** and thrown them **into prison.** He persecuted Christians even **to their death.** Paul probably had in mind the death of Stephen in particular, though he later referred more generally to several executions (26:10). The Jewish leaders could confirm Paul's claim because they had given him authority for his task. They had given him letters to fellow Jews in Damascus so Paul could go there, arrest Christians, and bring them back as prisoners to Jerusalem for punishment.

Verse 6: *"About noon as I came near Damascus, suddenly a bright light from heaven flashed around me.*

Paul began to describe in his own words what happened on the road to **Damascus.** As the apostle neared the end of his journey, *a bright light from heaven flashed around* him. This happened to Paul in broad day-light, *about noon* when the sun was at its brightest. Noting the time stressed the brightness of the *light.*

Verses 7-8: *I fell to the ground and heard a voice say to me, 'Saul! Saul! Why do you persecute me?'*

"'Who are you, Lord? I asked.

"I am Jesus of Nazareth, whom you are persecuting,' he replied.

Paul responded to this heavenly voice by asking the speaker to identi-fy Himself. The term **Lord** might have meant a polite *sir,* but Paul may have meant more than a mere word of respect. He did recognize the voice as that of a heavenly messenger and might have meant *Lord* in that sense.

Jesus answered the apostle and described Himself in two ways. First, as **Jesus of Nazareth.** Only here in the three conversion accounts do the words *of Nazareth* appear. This designation made clear to the Jewish crowd the precise identity of the One who spoke to Paul. Second, Jesus identified Himself as the One Paul was **persecuting.** In hounding Jesus' followers, Paul actually was persecuting the living Christ. Thus the Lord completely refuted all that Paul had been and done.

Verse 9: *My companions saw the light, but they did not understand the voice of him who was speaking to me.*

Paul interrupted his description of the conversation with the Lord to point out that his **companions saw the light** but did not hear the voice, that is, *understand the voice.* In Acts 9:7 Luke explained that Paul's companions heard the sound but did not see anyone. They saw the light but did not see the revelation of Jesus in glory. They heard the voice only as a noise, not as a message. The companions could verify that something unusual took place, but only Paul experienced the event as a divine revelation.

Verse 10: " *'What shall I do, Lord?' I asked.*

" *'Get up,' the Lord said, 'and go into Damascus. There you will be told all that you have been assigned to do.'*

The apostle responded naturally to the heavenly vision as a good Jew who thought first in terms of how he should act in obedience to divine revelation. *"What shall I do, Lord?"* Paul realized that he must now change his way of life. The **Lord** told him to **get up** and **go into Damascus** where he would receive instructions about what to do. At the beginning of his vision Paul might not have known whom he was addressing as *Lord.* Now he knew that it was Jesus, the risen Christ. Up to this point in his speech, Paul had identified closely with his Jewish listeners. He had presented himself to be as Jewish as they were in every way. Now Paul identified the new way his experience caused him to view Jesus. He testified that a faithful Jew could confess Jesus as Lord as he himself proved.

Verse 11: *My companions led me by the hand into Damascus, because the brilliance of the light had blinded me.*

The **brilliance of the light had blinded** him. Consequently, his **companions led** him **by the hand into Damascus.** Although his companions had seen the light and fallen to the ground, they evidently recovered immediately. Paul had to rely on others and wait for instructions as to God's purpose for him.

Verse 12: *"A man named Ananias came to see me. He was a devout observer of the law and highly respected by all the Jews living there.*

Ananias, a Jewish believer in Damascus, visited Paul. He served as God's messenger to bring about renewal of Paul's sight and to announce God's purpose for him as a witness to all people. Paul introduced Ananias as a pious Jew, a *devout observer of the law.* The Jewish community in Damascus *highly respected* him. Paul omitted the fact that Ananias was already a Christian disciple (9:10). That earlier account showed that Ananias was the link between the newly converted Paul and the Christian community. In Paul's testimony before the Jerusalem Jews, he emphasized Ananias's reputation as an upstanding Jew.

Verse 13: *He stood beside me and said, 'Brother Saul, receive your sight!' And at that very moment I was able to see him.*

With the word *Brother* Ananias recognized Paul's new relationship to Jesus Christ and to himself, not merely Paul's Jewish nationality. Paul immediately received his sight, confirming that what Ananias had to say to him was indeed a message from the Lord. After Paul could see again, Ananias delivered Christ's commission to him.

Ananias's words to Paul in 22:14-15 have a strong Jewish flavor. "God of our fathers" reflects the language of the Old Testament. The "Righteous One" is a Jewish messianic title. Paul wanted to emphasize that this pious Jew, who spoke in distinctly Jewish terms, communicated to Paul his commission from the risen Christ. The identification of the "God of our fathers" as the One calling Paul stressed to the crowd the continuity between the Old Testament revelation and the new revelation of God in Jesus. God Himself had chosen Paul to know His will, to see the Righteous One, and hear words from His mouth. He desired Paul to become a witness, declaring and proclaiming to all people—Jews and Gentiles—what he had seen and heard.

Verse 16: *And now what are you waiting for? Get up, be baptized and wash your sins away, calling on his name.'*

After delivering the Lord's message, Ananias called on Paul to respond, **What are you waiting for?** This common Greek idiom meant that the apostle needed to act on the Lord's commission. Ananias told Paul to identify himself with the community of believers by baptism. **Be baptized and wash your sins away** did not mean that the act of baptism would save Paul. His baptism was the outward and visible sign of his inward and spiritual cleansing from sin by the grace of God in Christ. Baptism portrayed God's grace provided through the death, burial, and resurrection of Christ (Rom. 6:4). The words **calling on his name** showed that Paul's profession of faith in Christ served as the basis for his baptism. Baptism also signified Paul's obedience to God's divine call.

Verse 17: *"When I returned to Jerusalem and was praying at the temple, I fell into a trance*

Paul concluded his testimony by telling of a vision he had **at the temple** in **Jerusalem.** Most likely this experience occurred on the apostle's return to Jerusalem, his first visit there three years after his conversion (9:26-30; Gal. 1:18-19). Christians continued to worship and pray in the temple. While Paul was worshiping there, he **fell into a trance**. Perhaps Paul referred to this event to indirectly answer the mob's charge that he had defiled the temple. One who went to the temple for prayer would not likely desecrate it.

Verse 18: *and saw the Lord speaking. 'Quick!' he said to me. 'Leave Jerusalem immediately, because they will not accept your testimony about me.'*

During his prayer in the temple, Paul **saw the Lord speaking.** Jesus commanded him to **leave Jerusalem immediately** for his own safety since the people would **not accept** his **testimony** about Him. This command to leave Jerusalem probably related to the conflict the apostle encountered in the synagogue of the Hellenistic Jews (9:29). Paul had debated with them. They were hostile toward him especially because they remembered his former zeal against the Christian movement. They saw him as a traitor. When he most needed God's guidance and support, the risen and exalted Jesus appeared to him again, directing him to leave Jerusalem.

Verse 19: *"'Lord,' I replied, 'these men know that I went from one synagogue to another to imprison and beat those who believe in you.*

Paul protested against the command to leave. He believed that he had convincing testimony to bear. The Jews surely would listen to the testimony of one who had imprisoned and beaten Christians in **one synagogue** after **another.** His former record would readily convince them that he based his change of attitude on the strongest reasons.

Verse 20: *And when the blood of your martyr Stephen was shed, I stood there giving my approval and guarding the clothes of those who were killing him.'*

Not only had Paul imprisoned and beaten believers, but he also had participated in Stephen's martyrdom. He had given his approval to this cruel event and guarded the clothes of **those who were killing him.** Surely these people must recognize that something dramatic had happened to change his life's direction. In reality, however, their knowledge of his former record made them all the more unwilling to hear him.

Verse 21: *"Then the Lord said to me, 'Go; I will send you far away to the Gentiles.'"*

The Lord's commandment, however, stood despite Paul's objection. **"Go."** Paul needed to depart from the holy city, not simply for his own safety but because God had another task for him. *I will send you far away to the Gentiles.* Paul's Gentile mission was thus connected closely to the refusal of the Jews to accept his witness to Christ.

During most of Paul's defense, the crowd listened with a certain respect. When Paul spoke, however, of God directing him by special revelation to leave Jerusalem and go *to the Gentiles,* they could tolerate no more. Basically Paul was saying that Gentiles could approach God directly without first being related to the Jewish nation, its laws, and traditions. This placed Jews and Gentiles on an equal footing before God. For Judaism this represented serious apostasy. The crowd interrupted Paul's speech at this point. They wanted to hear no more. So they shouted Paul down and called for his death, adding that he had no right even to exist.

In addressing the Jewish crowd in Jerusalem, Paul spoke first of his Jewish heritage and his role as a persecutor of Christians. In other words, (1) he described his life before Christ. Then he told about his encounter with Christ on the road to Damascus. (2) He stated how he became a believer. Finally, he related that the Lord had given him the task of preaching to the Gentiles. (3) He described how Christ had changed his life. In sharing our testimonies, we too may include these same elements. Each of us can ask ourselves these questions: What was my life like before I accepted the Lord Jesus Christ? How did I become a Christian? What difference has Jesus made in my life?

2. Paul Identified as a Roman Citizen (Acts 22:23-29)

The mob not only continued shouting negative things about Paul, but they also threw off their cloaks and flung dust into the air. These actions probably indicated they considered Paul a blasphemer and no longer a true Jew. The presence of the soldiers prevented further action against Paul. The crowd's outrage showed that Paul's life was in danger. Lysias, the commander, quickly ordered his troops to take Paul into the barracks. He still did not know why the people were rioting. Paul's address had not enlightened him because the apostle spoke in Aramaic.

Lysias decided to find out the truth of the matter by torturing Paul through flogging or scourging. This particularly cruel torture consisted of a beating across the raw flesh with leather thongs studded with pieces of metal or bone and fastened to a wooden handle. Its use often crippled for life and sometimes killed. Paul knew that as a Roman citizen he did not have to undergo such torture without due process. So as they stretched him out for the flogging, he wisely asked, "Is it legal for you to flog a Roman citizen who hasn't even been found guilty?" (22:25). The law prohibited the questioning of Roman citizens under torture by scourging. The centurion immediately halted the process and reported this new development to his commanding officer.

People highly valued Roman citizenship as a right conferred on those of high social or political standing, those who had done some special service for Rome, or those able to bribe some imperial or provincial administrator. No article of clothing distinguished a Roman citizen from the rest of the people except the toga, which only Roman citizens could wear. But even citizens in Rome rarely wore uncomfortable togas. Families kept papers proving their citizenship in family archives. The government had severe penalties for forging documents and making false claims of citizenship. How and when Paul's family acquired Roman citizenship is unknown. Probably one of Paul's ancestors received it for valuable services rendered to a Roman administrator or general.

Lysias noted that he had purchased his own citizenship for a large sum of money. The tribune did not doubt Paul's claim but was implying that anybody could become a citizen in those days. Paul replied that he was born a citizen. This meant that his father had been a Roman citizen before him. Paul's citizenship put the situation in a different light. The commander stopped the whole procedure. The fact that he even had placed Paul in chains alarmed him. He probably shuddered as he realized how close he had come to carrying out a serious offense against a Roman citizen. From this point on Lysias treated Paul with great respect.

3. Paul Before the Sanhedrin (Acts 22:30—23:11)

As a Roman citizen Paul had a right to know the nature of the charges against him and the penalties involved. The commander also needed to know these things in order to decide what further action to take. Since this was a religious matter, Lysias decided to turn to the Sanhedrin, the highest judicial body of Judaism. The commander released Paul from confinement so he could appear before the Jewish high court.

Before the Sanhedrin Paul asserted that he had fulfilled his duty to God in all good conscience to that day. If Paul's life as a Christian left him in complete innocence before God, then the members of the Jewish Sanhedrin who did not share his commitment to Christ were guilty. Paul's bold claim so enraged Ananias, the high priest, that he ordered those near the apostle to strike him on the mouth. Ananias reigned as high priest from A.D. 48 to 58 or 59. He had a reputation for greed and violence. He gave bribes to Romans and Jews. Jewish nationalists hated this brutal, scheming man for his pro-Roman policies.

Angry at this unjust treatment, Paul responded "God will strike you, you whitewashed wall!" (23:3). With these words the apostle accused the high priest of hypocrisy. The image referred to the practice of whitewashing tombs as a warning to people that the defilement of dead bones lay within. The character and actions of Ananias contradicted his role as high priest. Though Ananias sat in his role of judge, he himself needed judgment because his having Paul struck was clearly against the law. Jewish law protected the rights of defendants and presumed them innocent until proved guilty. Anyone who behaved as Ananias did would come under God's judgment. Paul's words, however, were prophetic. Ananias lived his final days as a hunted animal. He died at the hands of his own people—Jewish freedom fighters.

The members of the high council could not believe that Paul should call down a curse on "God's high priest." The emphasis on Ananias's being God's representative shifted the focus from the person to the office. So Paul apologized and cited Exodus 22:28 to emphasize he did respect God's leaders in accordance with the law. Either Paul really did not recognize that Ananias was the high priest, or he was speaking with irony. Paul had visited Jerusalem little during the past 20 years. The office of high priest had passed from one person to another. Ananias did not act as a high priest should act. How could Paul recognize him as such when he was so totally out of character?

Paul took the offensive. He stated what he saw as the real reason for this trial—his hope in the resurrection of the dead. Although Paul introduced the issue in general terms, he referred to the resurrection of Jesus. Some Bible students have seen Paul's words as a clever trick to divide the assembly and divert attention away from himself. The Sanhedrin consisted primarily of the high priestly aristocracy and the ruling elders who were primarily Sadducees. The scribes who sat in the Sanhedrin represented the Pharisees, the minority group. The Sadducees rejected the concepts of resurrection, angels, and spirits, while the Pharisees believed in them all. Paul deliberately made his appeal to the Pharisees in the Sanhedrin—but not in a deceitful way. He believed that the Pharisees' Judaism found its fulfillment in Christ (23:6-8).

Paul's mention of the resurrection sparked a dispute between the Pharisees and the Sadducees, dividing the assembly. Some of the Pharisees saw in the questioning of Paul an attempt by the Sadducees to discredit the Pharisees' theological views. Thus the Pharisees rose to the apostle's defense. They suggested that God might have spoken to Paul through a spirit or an angel. The dispute at this point became so violent that Lysias had to bring in soldiers and rescue Paul to keep them from tearing him to pieces (23:9-10).

After the mob in the temple square, the arrest, the attempted scourging, and the violence of the Sanhedrin, Paul might have despaired of ever fulfilling his plans to go to Rome and minister throughout the western part of the empire. What would happen next? The following night the risen and exalted Christ appeared to Paul, as He had done at other critical moments in his ministry. His presence encouraged Paul. The Lord assured him that a divine purpose existed in all that had happened to him. As he had testified in Jerusalem, so he would testify in Rome (23:11).

4. Plot to Kill Paul (Acts 23:12-22)

Paul needed the encouragement from the Lord's vision because more trouble awaited him. Failing in their earlier plot to kill Paul in the temple precincts, more than 40 fanatical Jews placed themselves under a vow to neither eat nor drink until they had killed Paul. They planned to ambush him in the narrow streets of Jerusalem as he was brought from the Fortress of Antonia north of the temple to the hall of the Sanhedrin southwest of the temple area. To lure him out of the fortress, they arranged with the chief priests and elders to ask for Paul's return before the Sanhedrin for further questioning. These men probably did not die of hunger or thirst since their vow would go unfulfilled. Jewish law provided for the release from a vow one could not fulfill because of unforeseen circumstances.

Somehow news of the plot reached the ears of Paul's nephew. As a

Roman citizen under protective custody, Paul could receive visitors. When Paul heard his nephew's warning, he asked one of the centurions to take the young man to the commander. Lysias sensed the importance of the matter and took the youth aside to hear about the matter in confidence. Paul's nephew reported in detail.

5. Paul Sent to Caesarea (Acts 23:23-35)

Not willing to risk having a Roman citizen killed while in his custody, the commander took steps quickly to move Paul to Caesarea. Felix, the governor of the province of Judea from A.D. 52-59, had established himself there. Lysias probably would have made this transfer sooner or later because the Jews were charging Paul with a capital crime. Only the governor had jurisdiction over such cases. So the commander ordered two centurions to get ready 200 infantry, 70 cavalry, and 200 spearmen for escort duty. He wanted them to leave for Caesarea that night.

For the first time in Acts, Luke provided the commander's name, Claudius Lysias. He drafted an official letter to Felix, summarizing the events from the riot in the temple precincts to the discovery of a plot against Paul's life. Lysias stretched the truth to his own benefit in claiming to have rescued Paul from the mob because he had learned of his Roman citizenship. He understood that the conflict was rooted in questions about Jewish law. His official report clearly stated that Paul had done nothing worthy of death or imprisonment—the Roman attitude throughout the apostle's imprisonment. Lysias also related that he had ordered Paul's accusers to prepare their case for presentation before Felix.

The soldiers carried out their orders and Paul was delivered safely to Caesarea. They handed both their prisoner and Lysias's letter to Felix. After reading the letter, Felix questioned Paul on the basis of its contents. On learning that Paul was from the Roman province of Cilicia, he felt competent as a provincial governor to hear the case himself. Until Paul's accusers arrived from Jerusalem, Felix confined Paul to the palace.

FOR FURTHER STUDY

1. Read "Baptism in the Early Church" in the Fall 1984 issue of *Biblical Illustrator.*
2. Read "Saul in Damascus" in the Spring 1993 issue of *Biblical Illustrator.*
3. Read "On the Road to Damascus" in the Fall 1995 issue of *Biblical Illustrator.*
4. See the article *"Caesarea by the Sea"* in the Winter 200 issue of *Biblical Illustrator.*

The Week of February 4

DALLYING WITH DESTINY

Background Passage: Acts 24:1—25:12
Lesson Passages: Acts 24:1,10-16,22-27

INTRODUCTION

"I don't want to do that right now." Some people respond in this way after they have heard a clear gospel presentation and have been asked if they want to receive God's gift of forgiveness and eternal life through Jesus Christ. Basically they do not want to repent. They do not want to ask Jesus to be the Boss of their lives. They want to live on their own terms and follow their own desires. In short, they are dallying with their eternal destiny. By putting off a decision for Christ, they are making the decision not to follow Him. They reject Christ and His offer of salvation.

This lesson presents Paul's defense before Felix and the apostle's later presentation of the gospel to Felix and Drusilla. The study emphasizes Felix's delaying a decision to respond positively to the gospel. It challenges us to develop answers to counter reasons people give for delaying to receive Christ.

Acts 24:1—25:12

1. Paul's Trial Before Felix (24:1-23)
2. Paul's Private Audience with Felix (24:24-27)
3. The Jews' Plot to Kill Paul (25:1-5)
4. Paul's Trial Before Festus and Appeal to Caesar (25:6-12)

THE BACKGROUND

When Paul returned to Jerusalem at the end of his third missionary journey, he participated in a ceremony in the temple for four Jewish believers who had taken a Nazirite vow. Some Asian Jews accused him falsely of defiling the temple. The resulting riot led to Paul's arrest and address to the crowd. On learning of a threat to Paul's life, the Romans moved him to Caesarea, the provincial capital, for protection. This lesson begins with the apostle's accusers arriving in Caesarea to press their charges against Paul before Felix, the governor.

The setting for the apostle's witnessing shifted from Jerusalem to

Caesarea. Paul testified there not to the Jewish religious leaders but to the social and political rulers of the holy land—the Roman procurators, Felix and Festus, and later the Jewish king, Agrippa II (25:23—26:32). In his account of Paul's defense before Felix, Luke gave almost equal space to the Jewish charges against Paul (24:1-9), Paul's reply to these charges (24:10-21), and Felix's response (24:22-27). He showed that despite the cleverness of the Jewish charges and the corruption of Felix, the governor probably could draw only two conclusions from Paul's appearance before him: (1) Christianity had nothing to do with political sedition and (2) Jewish opposition to Christianity sprang from the Christian claim that Jesus Christ fulfilled the hopes of Judaism.

Although the Roman officials became more and more convinced that Paul had broken none of their laws, they hesitated to release him because of the strong Jewish opposition. Only Paul's appeal to Caesar removed him from the strong possibility that the officials would ultimately give in to pressure and turn him over to the Jews.

THE LESSON PASSAGE

1. Paul's Trial Before Felix (Acts 24:1-23)

Verse 1: *Five days later the high priest Ananias went down to Caesarea with some of the elders and a lawyer named Tertullus, and they brought their charges against Paul before the governor.*

In his letter to Felix, Lysias had related that he was sending Paul's accusers to Caesarea to present their case before the governor (23:30). They arrived in the administrative capital *five days* after the apostle. The accusers consisted of the *high priest Ananias . . . some of the elders,* probably members of the Sanhedrin, *and a lawyer named Tertullus.* *Tertullus* was a common Greek name in the Roman world. He might have been a Hellenistic Jew, but he could have been a Gentile. Though Tertullus seemed to identify himself with the Jews by the use of "we" (24:2-8), Luke seems to have distinguished him from "the Jews" (24:9). As the Jews' attorney, he could have spoken as if he were one of them. Jews often hired pagan lawyers who knew more about Roman law than they did. Ananias surely had chosen Tertullus because of his expertise in Roman legal procedure.

Antonius Felix, the *governor,* was born a slave and freed by Antonia, the mother of the emperor Claudius. In A.D. 52 Claudius appointed him governor of Judea. During his governorship, revolts and lawlessness increased throughout the holy land. As he tried to put down the uprisings and regain control, his brutal methods alienated the Jewish population and led to further disturbances. Nero recalled Felix to Rome in A.D. 59.

After Felix called Paul in, Tertullus began the prosecution with a flattery designed to gain the governor's goodwill. The lawyer's words would have shocked many Jews, for he praised Felix for the peace that extended throughout the province (24:2). Actually, unrest had characterized Felix's administration, straining the relations between Rome and the Jews. Tertullus also praised Felix for his reforms or improvements in the Jewish nation. In truth, Felix had made life miserable for the Jews. Tertullus appealed further to Felix's vanity by claiming the Jews everywhere and in every way acknowledged his rule with gratitude. Few Jews would have felt gratitude for the governor's frequent displays of cruelty and greed. Nevertheless, Tertullus spoke in the manner expected of him. He also promised that he would speak briefly, as was the custom.

Luke probably provided only a summary of the lawyer's speech. First, the attorney identified Paul as a troublemaker who stirred up "riots among the Jews all over the world" (24:5). The word translated "troublemaker" literally meant a pest or plague. Tertullus cleverly was charging Paul with sedition, a charge the Romans would not take lightly. Roman officials would not involve themselves with matters of Jewish religion. They would take seriously, however, any threat to civil order. During his reign over Judea, Felix often had crucified the leaders of various uprisings and had killed many of their followers, maintaining the peace at any cost. Tertullus wanted to put Paul on the same level as these rebels, hoping that Felix would act in his usual manner simply on the basis of the testimony of the high priest and Jewish elders.

Second, the lawyer charged Paul with being the ringleader of the Nazarene sect. By linking this comment with the charge of provoking rebellion, Tertullus implied that the Christians as a whole were a dangerous and rebellious group, a revolutionary movement.

Third, the lawyer contended that Paul even tried to defile the temple, the center of Jewish piety and symbol of their nation. The Romans allowed the Jews the right to enforce their ban on Gentile access to their sacred precincts. They could impose the death penalty for this violation. Tertullus concluded his speech with an appeal to the governor to examine the evidence for himself. The Jews who were present joined in the accusations, asserting the truth of these charges. Tertullus, however, neither summoned any formal witnesses nor provided any solid evidence.

Verse 10: *When the governor motioned for him to speak, Paul replied: "I know that for a number of years you have been a judge over this nation; so I gladly make my defense.*

Rather than question Paul, the **governor motioned for him to speak.** Paul had no lawyer and spoke for himself. Like his opponent, the apostle also began with a flattering word. In contrast to Tertullus, however, Paul spoke more briefly and truthfully. He gladly appeared before *a judge* with such long experience in the country and who was aware of its customs. Felix had had contact with the Jewish nation for over a decade, first in Samaria and then as governor over the province of Judea.

Verse 11: *You can easily verify that no more than twelve days ago I went up to Jerusalem to worship.*

Paul dealt in turn with each charge made against him. First came the charge of stirring up rebellion. Paul had come to Jerusalem **no more than twelve days ago.** *Twelve days* did not provide enough time to organize a rebellion. Also he came not for political agitation but for **worship.** Felix could **verify** that Paul was worshiping, not inciting sedition, since the incident was still fresh in people's minds.

Verse 12: *My accusers did not find me arguing with anyone at the temple, or stirring up a crowd in the synagogues or anywhere else in the city.*

Paul had not argued with anyone or stirred up any **crowd**—not in the **temple** area, not in the Jewish **synagogues,** not **anywhere else in the city.** The Asian Jews had started the riot in the temple, not Paul.

Verse 13: *And they cannot prove to you the charges they are now making against me.*

Paul asserted that his accusers could not **prove** to the governor any of the **charges** they were **making against** him. They had no proof that would stand up in court.

Verse 14: *However, I admit that I worship the God of our fathers as a follower of the Way, which they call a sect. I believe everything that agrees with the Law and that is written in the Prophets,*

Paul had done none of the things his opponents alleged, yet he declared boldly what he actually did: he worshiped the **God of our fathers,** the ancestral God of Israel. Roman law gave him the freedom to do so. He worshiped God, however, **as a follower of the Way.** With these words Paul revealed the religious reason Ananias and the Jewish elders opposed him. Tertullus might have referred to the Christians as a **sect,** a party within Judaism that deviated from its basic tenets. Paul and his fellow believers, however, preferred to think of themselves as belonging to the *Way.* Theirs represented the true way of worshiping and serving the God of their Jewish ancestors. Paul's faith was not deviating from Judaism; it was at the center of the Jewish religion. He based his understanding of true religion on **everything that agrees with the Law and that is written in the Prophets**—the Old Testament Scriptures. The apostle regarded these as laying down the basis of Christian faith and practice as Jesus Himself claimed (Luke 24:27). Instead of merely defending himself, Paul gave a positive witness. He declared that the Way of Jesus Christ faithfully embraced and fulfilled Israel's national hope.

Verse 15: *and I have the same hope in God as these men, that there will be a resurrection of both the righteous and the wicked.*

Paul stated his conviction, based on his *hope in God,* that there would be a *resurrection* of the dead, including *both the righteous and the wicked.* At least the Pharisees shared this *same hope.* The Sadducees, such as the high priest Ananias, did not share this belief. Only in this passage did Paul assert the resurrection of all kinds of people. In his letters the apostle spoke only of a resurrection of the righteous, those who believe in Christ. This was probably because Paul wrote in a pastoral way to believers. The New Testament does speak of all persons being raised to face God's judgment (Matt. 25:31-46; John 5:28-29; Rom. 2:5-11). To mention the resurrection of the *wicked* implied the coming judgment. Even the Gentiles present, who might not understand the idea of the resurrection, had some understanding of judgment.

Paul realized the resurrection constituted the real point of disagreement with the Jews. He believed the same Scriptures, worshiped the same God, shared the same hope as they did. The resurrection of Christ separated the apostle and the other followers of the Way from the Jews and formed the key point of his witness.

Verse 16: *So I strive always to keep my conscience clear before God and man.*

Since Paul believed there would be a future judgment, he tried *always to keep* his *conscience clear before God and man.* A *clear* conscience meant one that did not condemn him, not because it was insensitive but because it could detect no wrong attitudes or actions. Paul believed himself blameless both in his duty to God and in his dealings with other people. Paul's wording reflected Jesus' summary of the law in terms of love of God and neighbor.

Paul responded to the third charge, that he had desecrated the temple, by summarizing for Felix what really had happened in Jerusalem. Paul had come to Jerusalem after an absence of several years. In the manner of a pious Jew who lived outside the holy land, he brought gifts for the poor and offerings. Luke mentioned the collection for the poor believers at Jerusalem for the first and only time in his Acts account (24:17). Paul's letters show that he devoted much time and effort to this relief gift and regarded its reception at Jerusalem as an important part of his work. The offerings probably referred to the payments made by Paul in behalf of the four Nazirites.

While Paul was ceremonially clean and participating in the ceremony for the four men, worshiping in the temple, Jews from Asia confronted him. Paul had no crowd of followers with him at the time nor had he done anything to create a disturbance.

The thought of these accusers angered Paul, as indicated by his breaking off in midsentence in the Greek text (24:19). They should have been in Caesarea and brought charges against the apostle face-to-face as

Roman legal procedure required. Instead, since they had no supporting evidence, the Asian Jews did not even show up at the trial. Roman law imposed heavy penalties on accusers who abandoned their charges. The disappearance of the accusers often meant the withdrawal of a charge. Their absence suggested they had nothing against Paul that would stand up in a Roman court of law. Paul had a solid reason for making this technical objection to the case against him. Tertullus had made an accusation with the total absence of witnesses for the prosecution, a serious breach of court procedure.

Paul had successfully shown that Tertullus's accusations lacked any supporting evidence. Paul had broken no Roman law or even Jewish religious law. He then pointed to the one genuine charge that the Jews could bring against him. The lawyer's own witnesses, the high priest and elders, had been present at Paul's hearing before the Sanhedrin. They could testify to the one issue that had surfaced in that hearing—Paul's belief in the resurrection of the dead. Paul, therefore, declared he was on trial because of this belief. Though most Jews shared this conviction in principle, Paul believed that the Messiah had come and the resurrection had begun in Jesus Christ.

Verse 22: *Then Felix, who was well acquainted with the Way, adjourned the proceedings. "When Lysias the commander comes," he said, "I will decide your case."*

Felix refused to give a verdict. After a decade in the holy land he was, to some extent, **well acquainted with the Way.** He could see that the Jewish charges against Paul were entirely religious in nature—even though presented in the guise of political rebellion. Luke used rather technical legal language to state that Felix **adjourned the proceedings.** This meant he refused to pass judgment until he had gathered further evidence.

Felix announced he would defer a decision until **Lysias the commander** came. In view of the conflicting statements made by Tertullus and Paul, perhaps Felix wanted further details from Lysias. Yet the commander already had sent his report, indicating clearly the whole case was a matter of Jewish religious law. Lysias had even stated that Paul had done nothing deserving of death or imprisonment. Felix, therefore, probably was not waiting for another report from Lysias. The governor simply was putting off the whole matter. He gave Ananias the deceptive promise of waiting for further testimony.

Felix did not want to pass a verdict, for the verdict surely would have been one of acquittal. He realized Paul was guilty of no crime by Roman law. He knew powerful Jews in this delegation were calling for Paul's condemnation. He did not want to make them angry. The facts of the case, however, meant he had to refuse to decide in favor of the Jewish authorities. So he in effect made no decision, leaving Paul in jail.

Verse 23: *He ordered the centurion to keep Paul under guard but to give him some freedom and permit his friends to take care of his needs.*

Meanwhile, Felix treated Paul in the manner appropriate to a Roman citizen against whom the court had not proved any crime. He **ordered the centurion to keep** the apostle **under guard** or in military custody. This gave Paul considerable freedom and allowed visitation from *friends.* His *friends* were his fellow Christians. They no doubt improved Paul's situation by supplying food and other necessities. Probably Paul and Ananias realized that Felix had no intention of making a decision on the case in the near future. They had to await the appointment of a new provincial governor before pressing for a resolution. They might have expected this new official soon, knowing the problem-filled nature of Felix's reign.

Paul responded to the false charges against him. We too should defend ourselves truthfully when others challenge our Christian character or ministry. Like Paul, we can turn adverse circumstances into opportunities for a positive witness.

2. Paul's Private Audience with Felix (Acts 24:24-27)

Verse 24: *Several days later Felix came with his wife Drusilla, who was a Jewess. He sent for Paul and listened to him as he spoke about faith in Christ Jesus.*

Having a Christian leader in custody gave Felix an opportunity to improve his fairly accurate knowledge of the Way. **Felix came with his wife Drusilla** to visit Paul. Felix's third wife, Drusilla, was the youngest daughter of Herod Agrippa I. At age 14 her brother Agrippa II married her to Azizus, the king of Emesa, a petty Syrian state. Felix determined to have this beautiful teenager for himself. Felix's status appealed to the unhappily married Drusilla. She left Azizus and married the procurator. As a Jew, she might have been the source of Felix's information on the Way. Whatever their motivation, they **sent for Paul and listened to him as he spoke** about the necessity of **faith in Christ Jesus.** The apostle took advantage of every opportunity to share the gospel.

Verse 25: *As Paul discoursed on righteousness, self-control and the judgment to come, Felix was afraid and said, "That's enough for now! You may leave. When I find it convenient, I will send for you."*

Paul did not spare Felix or his wife as he spoke about faith in Christ Jesus, for he spoke about **righteousness, self-control and the judgment to come.** Felix and Drusilla had not measured up to God's standards but had given in to their own lusts and greed. Their lives were characterized not by *righteousness* or *self-control* but by self-indulgence. Paul, consequently, focused on the prospect of the coming *judgment,* highlighting their need of salvation in Christ.

Felix had enough conscience left to feel fear at Paul's Christian message. A skeptic would have dismissed the apostle's reference to the judgment as fantasy, but not Felix. He genuinely was *afraid.* Felix dismissed Paul until a more *convenient* time, telling the apostle he would *send for* him. For the present he did not want to hear about personal morality and responsibility. He had no intention of repenting.

Verse 26: *At the same time he was hoping that Paul would offer him a bribe, so he sent for him frequently and talked with him.*

Felix sent for the apostle frequently, *hoping that Paul would* take the hint and *offer him a bribe* in exchange for his freedom. The governor must have thought Paul had access to some money. Perhaps he had heard of the relief offering Paul had delivered to the believers in Jerusalem. Perhaps his visiting friends would bring such an offering to Paul, who in turn would offer it to Felix. A Roman governor had the authority to defer deciding a case, but he also could speed it along if he chose to do so. Roman law prohibited taking bribes, but that law often was broken.

Verse 27: *When two years had passed, Felix was succeeded by Porcius Festus, but because Felix wanted to grant a favor to the Jews, he left Paul in prison.*

Felix continued to delay a decision in Paul's case. He kept Paul *in prison* for *two years* to *grant a favor to the Jews.* He knew there was no legitimate case against the apostle, so he did not want to turn him over to the Jews. Yet Felix feared the power of the Jewish leaders, so he would not free the apostle. Delaying the case or releasing Paul were the only legal options open to him. Keeping Paul in prison was the safe way out for the governor. Felix may have rationalized Paul's imprisonment as protection for the Christian missionary as well as a favor to the Jews.

Finally Rome removed Felix from office. He paid the consequences for his rule's corruption and brutality. His downfall came through an outbreak of hostilities between Jews and Greeks at Caesarea. The Jews claimed civil rights in the city because of their greater numbers, wealth, and the fact that Herod the Great, a Jew, had rebuilt the city. The Gentiles claimed control because they had the support of the military. They also contended the city was always meant to be a Gentile city. Felix used military force against the Jews, killing many, imprisoning others, and plundering their wealth. A delegation of Jews went to Rome to complain about his actions. Rome recalled Felix, replacing him with *Festus* in A.D. 60.

New procurators generally tried to dispose quickly of cases the previous governor left behind. They often released prisoners. With Festus's coming, perhaps Paul thought his case would soon find a favorable resolution. This did not happen.

Let us consider how to encourage individuals who put off receiving Christ. A decision to delay is a decision not to receive Him. Felix spoke of a convenient time, but that was an excuse to hide his reluctance to turn from his sinful lifestyle (see John 3:19-21). Our responsibility is to present a positive witness, sowing the gospel and leaving the results to God. Some will refuse Christ, but that is not a cause for our feeling guilty. Not everyone responded to the appeals of Paul or of Jesus Himself.

3. The Jews' Plot to Kill Paul (Acts 25:1-5)

The Jewish population of the holy land probably welcomed Porcius Festus as the successor to Felix. The situation demanded immediate action to deal with the troubles and tension left by Felix's poor leadership. Therefore Festus took only three days to settle in at Caesarea before going up to Jerusalem, the religious and cultural center of the people under his jurisdiction. Almost immediately the chief priests and Jewish leaders began to pressure Festus about Paul. Counting on the new governor's inexperience, the Jewish authorities requested Festus to transfer Paul's case to Jerusalem for trial. They wanted a chance to ambush and murder Paul. Earlier 40 zealous Jews asked the Sanhedrin to help them ambush Paul. Now the Jewish leaders themselves plotted his death.

Festus saw no reason to transfer Paul to Jerusalem. If the Jews felt the case so urgent, they could make the effort to come to the capital. Festus suggested that a responsible delegation should accompany him to Caesarea where they formally could bring their charges against Paul. Any hearing thus would have to take place under a Roman tribunal.

4. Paul's Trial Before Festus and Appeal to Caesar (Acts 25:6-12)

Festus returned to Caesarea. Paul's Jewish accusers evidently accepted the new governor's invitation and accompanied him. Festus convened court and ordered Paul brought before him, reopening the case against the apostle. The Jewish accusers restated their charges against Paul. Yet again they produced no witnesses, nor could they prove their charges. Luke did not specify their charges, but Paul's response indicated they were the same as those directed at him earlier. Paul insisted on his innocence and denied the charges one by one. He had done nothing against Jewish or Roman law.

As in the case of the trial before Felix, the matter ought to have ended with Paul's acquittal. Perhaps Festus thought the court would uncover more evidence if a trial took place in Jerusalem, the scene of the alleged crime. He did not have pure motives, however; he wanted to grant the Jews a favor. Festus, as Felix, saw in the case an opportunity to become popular with the Jews. He, therefore, asked the apostle whether he was willing to go and stand trial at Jerusalem. Festus assured Paul that he would not hand him over to Jewish jurisdiction. In Jerusalem he would have a Roman trial before the governor himself.

By custom a Roman judge would set up a group of advisers to aid him in coming to a decision. Probably Festus would use some representatives of the Sanhedrin on his judicial council. Paul knew he would not have neutral advisers from the Jews in Jerusalem. He understood that to return to Jerusalem was to place himself in serious danger. Once he was there, the Jewish authorities would pressure Festus to have him turned over to them for trial on the charge of profaning the temple. This carried the death penalty.

Paul responded with some defiance. He insisted that the present court, a Roman one, should judge him. He rebuked the procurator when he told him that Festus knew very well that Paul had not wronged the Jews in any way. Paul knew that he would have no hope if surrendered to Jewish jurisdiction. Only under a Roman tribunal could he hope for any justice.

Thus Paul went on to claim one final right he had as a Roman citizen, an appeal to Caesar. A citizen of Rome living in the provinces could appeal to Caesar for trial by an imperial court at Rome in particular cases, namely those not involving well-established precedent or where the threat of violence or capital punishment existed. Why would Paul want to appeal to the harsh Nero? Although Nero later persecuted the Christians in Rome, Paul's case occurred in the earlier years of Nero's reign. His dark side had not yet appeared.

Paul assured Festus that he did not wish to go around the law or escape the due penalty of anything he might have done. If the Jewish charges had no substance, the governor must not place him in the Jews' power. Paul's appeal probably relieved Festus. It took the politically tricky case out of his hands, providing a way of escape from a difficult and dis-agreeable situation. Such an appeal did not happen regularly, so Festus turned to his council before giving formal acknowledgment. He then will-ingly granted this Christian Roman citizen permission to have his case referred to Rome. At last, Paul would be able to bear his witness in Rome.

FOR FURTHER STUDY

1. Read "Porcius Festus" in the Summer 1978 issue of *Biblical Illustrator.*

2. Read "Felix and Drusilla" in the Summer 1979 issue of *Biblical Illustrator.*

3. See the article "Roman Law" in the *Holman Bible Dictionary,* page 1200.

4. See "Caesarea by the Sea" and "A Supreme Court Appeal" in the Winter 2000 issue of *Biblical Illustrator.*

The Week of February 11

RESPONDING TO THE GOSPEL

Background Passage: Acts 25:13—26:32
Lesson Passages: Acts 26:15-23,26-32

INTRODUCTION

"What does it mean to be a Christian?" I rejoiced inwardly as a preteen girl asked me that question. This made all the trying moments of serving as camp counselor worthwhile. Together we looked at the page in her camp notebook that clearly presented the gospel message. The girl and several of her friends asked questions. During a service later that week, two of those girls responded to the pastor's invitation to receive Jesus Christ as Savior. They had made the most important decision a person must ever make. They responded positively to the gospel.

This lesson focuses on Paul's witness to Agrippa. The study challenges us to respond positively to the gospel by receiving Christ as Savior. If we are already believers, let us thank God for our salvation in Christ.

Acts 25:13—26:32
1. Festus's Consultation with Agrippa (25:13-22)
2. Paul's Appearance Before Agrippa (25:23-27)
3. Paul's Testimony to Agrippa (26:1-23)
4. Paul's Appeal to Agrippa (26:24-29)
5. Paul's Innocence Declared (26:30-32)

THE BACKGROUND

Paul's defense before Herod Agrippa II consisted of another account of his conversion experience and commission from Christ. The apostle presented his Christian position in relation to Judaism, stressing that his Christian faith matched his Jewish beliefs as a Pharisee. Paul also emphasized that his commission from the risen Lord included the offer of salvation both to Jews and Gentiles. He then gave his most complete exposition of the theme of the resurrection. He wanted everyone to know that his commitment to the risen Christ was the reason for his imprisonment. Paul's testimony before Agrippa fulfilled Jesus' commission to him that he would witness before kings (9:15).

1. Festus's Consultation with Agrippa (Acts 25:13-22)

Within days of Paul's appeal to Caesar, King Agrippa and his younger sister, Bernice, arrived at Caesarea. As ruler of the neighboring kingdom to the north, Herod Agrippa II came to pay his respects to Festus, the new governor of Judea. Herod Agrippa II was the son of Herod Agrippa I, whose death was described in Acts 12, and the great-grandson of Herod the Great. The Roman emperors Claudius and Nero had granted him various territories northeast of the holy land. Agrippa ruled over these primarily Gentile regions with the status of a king. Roman procurators governed the main Jewish territories of Judea, Samaria, and Galilee. The Romans did grant Agrippa the custody of the ceremonial vestments worn by the high priest on the Day of Atonement and gave him the authority to appoint the high priest. With these privileges the Romans considered him to be the king of the Jews and an authority on the Jewish religion.

Bernice and Agrippa were rumored to have an incestuous relationship. Married at 13 and widowed at a young age, she was Agrippa's companion for a number of years.

Since the Jews' charges against Paul primarily concerned Jewish religious matters, Festus mentioned Paul's case to Agrippa during his visit. The procurator gave his own version of the events reported in 25:1-12. Though the Jewish leaders wanted Paul condemned without a fair trial, Festus acted in accordance with Roman law in demanding they make charges properly and confront the apostle face-to-face. The law allowed Paul to answer their charges. As Lysias did earlier (23:27-30), Festus tried to show himself in the most favorable light, even if that meant bending the truth a little. He wanted to appear efficient as the new procurator.

Festus told Agrippa that the Jews did not charge Paul with any of the crimes he expected, such as treason or breaking other Roman laws. Instead, their charges only dealt with matters of their own religion and a "dead man named Jesus who Paul claimed was alive" (25:19). In an effort to resolve the situation, the procurator told Agrippa he had considered transferring the case to Jerusalem. Paul had refused and claimed his right of appeal to the emperor, which Festus had granted.

The procurator's report stirred Agrippa's curiosity. He asked to hear Paul, and Festus promised to arrange a meeting for the next day.

2. Paul's Appearance Before Agrippa (Acts 25:23-27)

Agrippa and Bernice entered the audience room of Herod the Great's Caesarean palace "with great pomp" (25:23), signifying the pageantry of a state occasion. A procession of high ranking officers, probably tribunes, and the leading men of the city accompanied them. After their impressive entrance, Festus commanded the guards to bring in Paul.

Festus introduced the prisoner by providing a summary of the events related to the apostle's case. For Festus it had begun with a petition from the Jews seeking Paul's death. The governor then explained to his important guests how Paul had appealed to Caesar. Festus himself had found that Paul had done nothing deserving of death. Since Paul made his appeal to the emperor, however, Festus decided to send him to Rome.

The governor needed to list definite charges against Paul in his report to the emperor, but he did not know what to include. He was allowing Paul to speak before this important group in the hope that they would help him draw up the charges. He particularly asked for Agrippa's advice since he knew more about Jewish matters. Actually the emperor would consider the failure to specify charges a neglect of duty. That perhaps could end the governor's career.

3. Paul's Testimony to Agrippa (Acts 26:1-23)

Paul's defense before Agrippa was directed to a distinguished audience. He framed his testimony to appeal particularly to the king.

King Agrippa formally granted Paul permission to speak. Though bound by chains, the apostle was able to gesture with his hands in the manner typical of ancient orators.

Paul "began his defense" (26:1) with the customary attempt to gain the favor of King Agrippa. He expressed appreciation for the opportunity to speak and complimented the king, who was well acquainted with all the Jewish customs. He would understand the Jews' accusations as well as Paul's response. Agrippa also had a Greek background and lived a Roman lifestyle. His unique position enabled him to give his opinion on both the Jewish and Roman legal aspects of Paul's situation. Agrippa indeed could judge the apostle's case far better than Festus. Paul asked the king to listen to him patiently, implying a fairly lengthy statement.

The apostle began his testimony by describing his strict Jewish upbringing that was well-known to his accusers. He had spent his life among his people in his own country of Cilicia and in Jerusalem. He had lived as a Pharisee, the strictest sect of the Jewish religion. As he had done before the Sanhedrin, Paul stressed that his background as a Pharisee closely related to his hope in God's promises to the fathers of the Jewish nation. "Hope" referred to believing and expecting that God would fulfill the promises and prophecies made in the Old Testament, particularly those pertaining to the Messiah. Paul believed Jesus and His resurrection fulfilled these promises of Israel's hope.

The Jews believed earnestly in this hope. In their worship they prayed for its fulfillment day and night. All twelve tribes—all of Israel—shared this hope. Paul could not understand why the Jews who prayed and hoped to see the fulfillment of God's promises would accuse him because he believed these promises had now been realized in Christ. He took the offensive by addressing the whole crowd in the audience chamber. He asked why any of them would find it unbelievable that God should raise the dead. Although Paul asked the question in general terms, he really referred to the resurrection of Jesus that proved He was the Messiah. This was the real issue behind his trial.

Paul had interrupted his personal testimony to speak of his hope. Then he continued. Earlier he also had persecuted the Christians. He described it as opposing the name of Jesus of Nazareth (26:9), whom he considered a blasphemer and heretic. He attacked believers in Jerusalem. Acting with the authority of the chief priests, Paul put Christians in prison. He agreed with the death penalty for their heresy, giving his consenting vote when the Christians were condemned to death. He had believers punished in the local synagogues and attempted to make them "blaspheme" (26:11, spoken from Paul's present view of Jesus as the Christ), to denounce Jesus as a pretender. He even pursued them in the cities outside of the holy land.

While Paul was trying to stamp out the new Christian movement, the risen Christ confronted him on the road to Damascus. The life of the former persecutor of Christians changed. For the third time in Acts we read of Paul's conversion (9:1-30; 22:3-21). Paul related his experience basically the same as in the two prior accounts but with several differences. He did not mention his blindness or the visit of Ananias. He noted that the heavenly light was brighter than the sun and that it blazed around both him and his companions. Paul stated that his traveling companions also fell to the ground at the appearance of the brilliant light. Only here did Paul say that the heavenly voice spoke in Aramaic.

All three testimony accounts relate the question the risen Christ asked Paul, "Why do you persecute me?" Only in this final account did Paul add the further words of the Lord, "It is hard for you to kick against the goads." This proverb from agricultural life was common among the Greeks and Romans. Paul's Gentile audience would have understood the words to mean resisting one's destiny or fighting the will of the gods. In opposing Christ, Paul was fighting God's will. Like a beast of burden kicking against his master's prodding sticks, he would only find the blows more severe with each successive kick.

Verse 15: *"Then I asked, 'Who are you, Lord?'*
" 'I am Jesus, whom you are persecuting,' the Lord replied.

In response to Paul's question, the heavenly speaker identified Himself only as **Jesus.** Paul did not need to identify *Jesus* more precisely as being from Nazareth as he did when addressing the Jews before the temple. Jesus described Himself as the one **whom** Paul was **persecuting.** By attacking the Christians, Paul was persecuting the Lord Himself. Paul implicitly identified Jesus as the **Lord.** If Jesus addressed him in this way from heaven, it proved that God had exalted Him to a position of authority alongside Himself.

Verse 16: *'Now get up and stand on your feet. I have appeared to you to appoint you as a servant and as a witness of what you have seen of me and what I will show you.*

Paul emphasized the commission given to him by the risen Jesus (26:16-18). The words Christ used to appoint Paul recalled the commissioning of Old Testament prophets. The Lord commanded Paul to **get up and stand on his feet** (see Ezek. 2:1). From previous accounts we know the Lord told Paul to go into the city and there receive further instruction. Here, however, Paul condensed the story. He communicated correctly what God said to him through Ananias and in the temple when he returned to Jerusalem (Acts 22:21), though omitting the details. The apostle's obedience to Christ's command had led to the way of life for which he now stood on trial.

Jesus **appeared** to him in order **to appoint** him **as a servant and as a witness.** *Servant* emphasized his subservient relationship to his Lord. As servant, he would work for his Master, obediently following His instructions. As *witness,* he would bear testimony to **what** he had **seen** of Christ and **what** Christ would **show** him.

Verse 17: *I will rescue you from your own people and from the Gentiles. I am sending you to them*

The promise to rescue Paul from all enemies also characterized the call of Old Testament prophets (Jer. 1:8). God's promise applied to the safe fulfillment of his ministry and not necessarily to his physical life. Later Paul would write of suffering for the gospel and wearing chains like a criminal. Tradition holds that he eventually was executed for his faith.

The Lord announced that He was **sending** Paul to Jews and Gentiles. The word *apostle* means one who is sent. God sent the Old Testament prophets too (Jer. 1:7; Ezek. 2:3). The objective of Paul's mission follows.

Verse 18: *to open their eyes and turn them from darkness to light, and from the power of Satan to God, so that they may receive forgiveness of sins and a place among those who are sanctified by faith in me.'*

The risen Christ defined Paul's assignment in words based on the description of the Servant's task in Isaiah 42:6-7. As God's righteous Servant, Jesus Christ is actually the One who opens the eyes of those in **darkness** and brings **light** to the nations. The Lord called Paul to participate in this redemptive ministry. The Holy Spirit would work through the apostle to **open . . . eyes** blinded by sin, bringing people out of the realm of *darkness* into that of *light.* This is further described as turning *from the power of Satan to God. Light* represents life in Christ, a life marked by righteousness and directed by God, not by self. *Darkness* symbolizes living according to the world, under Satan, in sin, apart from God, and totally self-centered.

Paul ended his summary of the gospel mission by citing two results that come to those who respond to Christ in faith. First, they receive *forgiveness of sins.* This removes the barrier that separates them from God. The restoring of fellowship with God clears the way for the second result—assurance of a *place* in God's eternal kingdom, *among those who are sanctified by faith* in Christ. Believing Gentiles would have an equal and rightful share in the heritage of the holy people of God. Though Paul proclaimed the gospel to the Jews, proclaiming the gospel to the Gentiles was his special mission.

Verse 19: *"So then, King Agrippa, I was not disobedient to the vision from heaven.*

The risen and glorified Jesus had confronted Paul. From this point on he knew but one Master. He acknowledged this to **King Agrippa,** saying he **was not disobedient** to the heavenly **vision.** Indeed, he obeyed it enthusiastically and immediately. He became the Lord's servant and witness.

Verse 20: *First to those in Damascus, then to those in Jerusalem and in all Judea, and to the Gentiles also, I preached that they should repent and turn to God and prove their repentance by their deeds.*

After his conversion Paul immediately began to proclaim Jesus as the Son of God to the Jews **in Damascus, then to those in Jerusalem** and elsewhere, and especially **to the Gentiles.** This fits Paul's missionary pattern of beginning in the synagogue before turning to the Gentiles. Paul had preached in *Damascus* after his conversion and later in Jerusalem (9:20-30). Luke's record does not mention the larger witness **in all Judea.**

As he had done throughout his speech, Paul did not pass up any opportunity to declare the gospel to the king. So in speaking of his witness to Jews and Gentiles, he included the content of his preaching—*that they should repent and turn to God.* Repenting and turning to God express the same act. True repentance means a complete change of mind, a turn from the world, sin, and self to God. Paul also preached that those who so turned to God would *prove their repentance by their deeds.* A life characterized by good works gives proof of the genuineness of repentance and faith. Works do not serve as the basis of salvation. They result as the natural fruit of a true experience of turning to God in Christ.

Verse 21: *That is why the Jews seized me in the temple courts and tried to kill me.*

Paul's preaching to Gentiles was behind the Jew's violent opposition to Paul. They seized him **in the temple courts and tried to kill** him on the spot. Their efforts had failed. Knowing the Jews as he did, surely Agrippa understood why they hated a former colleague who offered Gentile believers spiritual privileges on the same footing as God's chosen people.

Verse 22: *But I have had God's help to this very day, and so I stand here and testify to small and great alike. I am saying nothing beyond what the prophets and Moses said would happen—*

Roman intervention had saved Paul from the hands of the Jews, yet behind this human protection lay the hand of God. In fulfillment of Christ's promise Paul had *God's help* right up to the present moment. The Lord had protected him and enabled him to *testify to small and great alike.* Paul observed no geographical, racial, or social barriers in his witness. All ranks of society had received his testimony—kings, governors, and common folk. Finally, Paul emphasized that all of his preaching and teaching was completely loyal to Israel's faith and in total harmony with *what the prophets and Moses said would happen.* The Jews, therefore, should have accepted his witness, namely:

Verse 23: *that the Christ would suffer and, as the first to rise from the dead, would proclaim light to his own people and to the Gentiles."*

Paul gave the Old Testament basis of the gospel. First, the *Christ would suffer,* that is, die. Paul identified the Messiah as the Suffering Servant (Isa. 53). The Jews no doubt disputed this connection. No evidence indicates that pre-Christian Judaism ever thought of the Messiah in terms of suffering. Second, the Messiah would be the *first to rise from the dead* and would *proclaim light* both to *his own people,* the Jews, and *to the Gentiles.* Paul's statement reflects the Christian teaching that Jesus is the firstfruits of the resurrection (1 Cor. 15:20). Again Paul identified Jesus as the Servant who would proclaim light to all people (Isa. 49:6).

Luke did not give Paul's citation of messianic texts in the summary of his speech before Agrippa. He had included these from Peter's sermons at Pentecost (Acts 2:14-41) and before the temple crowd (3:11-26) and from Paul's sermon in the synagogue of Pisidian Antioch (13:16-48). Jesus Himself had provided His disciples with the scriptural base for their understanding of His death and resurrection.

Ultimately the role of witness is the key role for every disciple. All of us who have encountered the risen Christ are commissioned to be His witnesses. When we share our salvation testimonies, we encourage unbelievers to consider seriously the claims of Christ. The gospel is relevant to all people regardless of their geographic, racial, or social backgrounds. We should allow no barrier to keep us from being faithful witnesses.

4. Paul's Appeal to Agrippa (Acts 26:24-29)

At this point Festus interrupted Paul's address. The apostle's reference to the resurrection made the governor shout out, "You are out of your mind, Paul!" (26:24). No sensible Roman could believe in the resurrection of a person from the dead. Even if he privately accepted such an unusual belief, he would not allow it to affect his practical living or bring him into danger of death. Festus concluded, therefore, that Paul's "great learning" had made him insane. This practical Roman official had no time for religious speculations. Paul politely addressed the governor as "most excellent Festus" and firmly insisted that what Festus declared to be madness was "true and reasonable" (26:25)

Verse 26: *The king is familiar with these things, and I can speak freely to him. I am convinced that none of this has escaped his notice, because it was not done in a corner.*

Festus had called the audience primarily so Agrippa could hear Paul. The apostle addressed the king directly throughout his speech (26:2,7,19). He now turned to King Agrippa for support. He claimed that *the king* understood what he was talking about. Therefore, he could *speak freely* to him, that is, with confidence. Agrippa knew the Jewish hope in the resurrection. He knew the Scriptures and understood what Paul meant when he referred to the prophets.

Paul was *convinced* that the Christian movement had not *escaped* the king's *notice, because it was not done in a corner. Not done in a corner* was another Greek idiom of the day. This expression often appeared in Greek philosophical writings, especially in contexts where others accused philosophers of withdrawing from society. The ministry of Jesus was widely known in the holy land. Agrippa would have heard of it. Also many attested to Jesus' death and resurrection. Paul's witness also had been fully public. He had proclaimed Christ and the resurrection to the Athenians on the Areopagus. He had stood before the city leaders of Philippi and before the proconsul Gallio in Corinth. He had preached to the Jewish crowd in the temple square and spoken before the Sanhedrin. Romans governors and the Jewish king himself had heard his testimony. Paul had done nothing in a secluded corner but openly to full public view.

Verse 27: *King Agrippa, do you believe the prophets? I know you do.*

The apostle spoke even more boldly to the king. The prisoner became the questioner as Paul fearlessly asked, *"King Agrippa, do you believe the prophets?"* If Agrippa was a worshiping Jew, he must surely have believed what the prophets said. Paul was thinking about the messianic prophecies such as those he already had mentioned. Anyone who believed the prophets and compared their predictions with the historical facts concerning Jesus must acknowledge the truth of Christianity. Paul wanted Agrippa to supply supporting testimony and assure Festus that his arguments were sane and well-founded since he was preaching what the prophets and Moses said would occur. Paul added, *I know you do* believe. At most he was suggesting that Agrippa believed that the prophets foretold the coming of the Messiah.

Verse 28: *Then Agrippa said to Paul, "Do you think that in such a short time you can persuade me to be a Christian?"*

Paul's direct appeal embarrassed Agrippa and put him in an awkward position. The king wanted to maintain his reputation before Festus and the other dignitaries. If he confessed belief in the prophets, Paul would press him for a commitment to Christ with the obvious follow-up question, "Then will you accept that Jesus is the Messiah?" On the other hand, he could not deny that he believed in the prophets. He would consequently lose his reputation for orthodoxy and his influence with the Jews. Whatever King Agrippa thought about Paul's message personally, he was too worldly wise to commit himself in public to what others thought was madness.

Agrippa evaded Paul's question with one of this own, *"Do you think that in such a short time you can persuade me to be a Christian?"* The king was removing himself from Paul's logical argument. The Greek adjective translated *in such a short time* also could be rendered "almost" (see the *King James Version*). Yet the translation relating to duration of time seems the more likely since Paul played on that idea in verse 29.

Verse 29: *Paul replied, "Short time or long—I pray God that not only you but all who are listening to me today may become what I am, except for these chains."*

Paul used the king's own words to indicate that the time needed to persuade Agrippa did not matter to him, whether **short time or long.** The apostle directed his appeal not only to the king but also to the other dignitaries. He expressed his prayer that not only Agrippa but also everyone hearing him would become a Christian. He wanted others to know the Lord Jesus, but not to share his *chains* or imprisonment.

A presentation of the gospel invites people to receive Christ. Have you responded to Christ's invitation to know Him? If you have, are you presenting His invitation to others?

5. Paul's Innocence Declared (Acts 26:30-32)

Verse 30: *The king rose, and with him the governor and Bernice and those sitting with them.*

Paul might have continued his witness; but the **king rose** to his feet, signaling the end of the session. When Agrippa stood, the **governor, Bernice,** and **those sitting** with them followed his example. Agrippa had heard enough to know that Paul had not broken any Roman law. The apostle was innocent. He also had heard enough of Paul's witness to know he was not ready to become a believer. He remained unpersuaded.

Verse 31: *They left the room, and while talking with one another, they said, "This man is not doing anything that deserves death or imprisonment."*

Agrippa, Festus, and the group with them discussed among themselves what Paul had said. They agreed that he had done nothing deserving **death** or even **imprisonment.** Agrippa could now offer Festus advice on what he should write in his report to Rome. This was the fifth time others had declared Paul's innocence (23:9,29; 25:18,25).

Verse 32: *Agrippa said to Festus, "This man could have been set free if he had not appealed to Caesar."*

If Paul had done nothing to deserve death or imprisonment, why was he not freed immediately? Felix and Festus had refused to do so for the sake of political expediency—to gain favor with the Jews. Agrippa commented that Paul could *have been set free* then and there *if he had not appealed to Caesar.* Agrippa's remark indicated that stopping the appeal process would not be easy. In strict law, acquittal at this stage would have been possible; but to acquit Paul would have offended the emperor and admitted Festus's incompetence in allowing the process to be set in motion. Paul had long desired to go to Rome and proclaim the gospel. He might have reached Rome in other ways. By going to appear before the emperor, however, he might have hoped to serve as a test case and receive a decision giving toleration to Christianity.

When unbelievers hear the gospel, they have an immediate opportunity to repent of their sins and receive Christ by faith. Let's make certain they hear the gospel.

FOR FURTHER STUDY:

1. Read "Herod Agrippa II" in the Winter 2000 issue of *Biblical Illustrator.*

2. Read the article on "Bernice" in the *Holman Bible Dictionary,* 166.

3. Read the article on "Herod" in the *Holman Bible Dictionary,* 639-40.

The Week of February 18
TRUSTING GOD'S PROMISES

Background Passage: Acts 27:1-44
Lesson Passages: Acts 27:18-26,33-36,44b

INTRODUCTION

I already had completed two years of seminary study. As I started another spring semester, my bank balance after registration and buying books came to about eleven dollars, a figure I well remember. School expenses for the year had wiped out my previous summer's earnings. Though I had a work scholarship, the program did not give me any money directly; it provided for my room and board on campus. I wondered how I would buy any personal items for the coming months. My prayer partner and I prayed and claimed God's promises to supply my needs. I knew He had called me to seminary and He would enable me to finish. Shortly after the beginning of classes for that term, a professor asked me to serve as his grader for the semester. I agreed, and the school refunded my tuition—the pay for graders! My bank account improved by hundreds of dollars. God had kept His promises.

This lesson focuses on God's promise to Paul that he would arrive safely in Rome and that no lives would be lost during the storm and shipwreck. The study emphasizes Paul's firm trust in God's promises and his encouraging others to believe in God. It challenges us to trust God's promises and to encourage others in difficult times.

Acts 27:1-44

1. Sailing for Rome (27:1-12)
2. Facing a Storm (27:13-20)
3. Encouraging Words (27:21-26)
4. Surviving Shipwreck (27:27-44)

THE BACKGROUND

Acts provides an extensive narrative of Paul's sea voyage from Caesarea to Rome to appear before Caesar. Luke often presented Paul's voyages in great detail, naming ports, landmarks, and even time spent in sailing (for example, 21:1-8). Acts 27 provides precise details of first-century seamanship and of conditions on the eastern Mediterranean. The story of Paul's voyage to Rome contains the longest "we passage" in Acts.

Luke was an eyewitness of the events of this voyage and vividly presented the memorable, trying experiences. Luke's detailed treatment of the shipwreck narrative emphasizes its theme—the providence or care and protection of God. At each point when the situation seemed desperate, Paul offered a word of encouragement from God. The apostle warned the sailors of disaster, encouraged them in times of danger, and helped save the lives of the crew and passengers. God delivered Paul and all who sailed with him; Paul's ultimate purpose was to bear witness before Caesar.

THE LESSON PASSAGE

1. Sailing for Rome (Acts 27:1-12)

Festus made arrangements to place Paul and other prisoners in the custody of a centurion named Julius, who belonged to the Imperial Regiment. He might have belonged to the auxiliary cohort stationed in Caesarea, or he might have served as a special officer representing the emperor and not attached to a particular legion.

At Caesarea, Julius, a group of soldiers, and the prisoners boarded a coastal vessel from the city of Adramyttium, a seaport of Mysia on the northwest coast of Asia Minor, southeast of Troas. Coasting vessels traveled close to shore and put in at the various ports along the way. The Adramyttium ship was probably returning to its home port. Julius evidently intended to transfer to a ship sailing to Rome at one of the ports along the way. The ports of southern Asia offered a good opportunity for finding such a vessel. Luke and Aristarchus, a Macedonian from Thessalonica, embarked with Paul. As a Roman citizen who had appealed to the emperor, Paul had a more favored position than the other prisoners. The passenger list might have entered his two companions as his personal doctor and servant.

The Adramyttium coasting vessel sailed some 70 miles north to the old Phoenician port of Sidon. There the boat either loaded or unloaded cargo. Boats could spend much time doing this task whenever they put into a harbor. Ordinary passengers would go ashore to pass the time. The centurion showed kindness to Paul by letting him go ashore, presumably with a soldier as a guard. Paul evidently had made a good impression on Julius, who trusted him and held him in high esteem. The "friends" the apostle visited were the Christians of Sidon (27:3). They provided for Paul's needs, probably furnishing food and supplies for the voyage. In those days passengers often had to provide such necessities for themselves.

After leaving Sidon, the ship sailed to the leeward side of Cyprus, that is, the sheltered eastern coast of the island away from the winds. The vessel kept close to the coast and took advantage of the night breezes from the shore. After it rounded Cyprus, the ship had to make its way through the open sea, bearing north to the coast of Cilicia and Pamphylia. The offshore winds and the current that ran along the shoreline enabled the boat to make its westerly course until it came to Myra, a seaport in Lycia, the southernmost part of Asia.

At Myra Julius arranged with the owner of a larger Alexandrian grain ship to take the soldiers and prisoners on board for the longer voyage to Italy. Although such vessels had private owners, they received special consideration from the Roman government in view of their importance in providing food. Grain ships were usually quite large. An important trade route existed from Egypt to Italy, bringing grain for the vast population of Rome. Since ancient ships were not well designed for sailing against the wind, ships from Alexandria sailed north to Myra. From there they took advantage of the coast of Asia Minor for the next stage of the journey and then sailed north of Crete to Sicily.

Presumably the Alexandrian ship set out hoping to reach Italy before wintry conditions made sailing impossible. Yet at the beginning of the voyage from Myra the elements began to hinder its progress. The grain ship moved westward only with great difficulty and took a long time to reach Cnidus, a peninsula forming the southwest tip of Asia Minor between the islands of Cos and Rhodes. The normal route from Myra would have taken the vessel south of Rhodes, from there south to Crete, and then along the northern coast of that island. The northern winds that blew down from the Aegean Sea at that time of year pushed the ship off course and forced the pilot to seek protection along the southern leeward coast of Crete, the long island southeast of Greece. Passing Cape Salmone on the eastern tip of Crete, the ship continued westwards on the south side of the island. With difficulty the vessel reached the first convenient shelter, the small bay of Fair Havens near the town of Lasea.

The ship had lost valuable time since leaving Myra. Sailing had already become dangerous because by now it was after the "Fast" (27:9), the Day of Atonement, which fell in late September or early October. Travel in that part of the Mediterranean was dangerous after mid-September. After early November such travel ceased altogether and did not begin again until the beginning of February at the earliest. At this point Paul gave his warning that there would be loss both of cargo and of life if they continued on their journey. The apostle based his advice on the well-known facts of both the time of year and the actual presence of bad weather. Any travel at that time would be dangerous. Luke did not indicate whether Paul was making an inspired prophecy or simply giving his opinion. Nor did he make clear to whom Paul spoke. Since Julius treated the apostle with consideration as a Roman citizen under arrest but not yet convicted of any crime, Paul likely felt free to express his opinions to the centurion and even to the officers of the ship. The limited space of the ship would not keep the officers, crew, and passengers separated from one another.

Luke showed the centurion as the person of authority aboard the ship. Although the owner of the vessel itself was on board, he served as a contractor for the state transport of grain. The centurion, however, as the highest official on board, ranked as commanding officer since the ship was in service to the state.

Julius deferred to the expert knowledge of sailing conditions on the part of the owner and his pilot. These sailing professionals preferred not to winter in the small open bay of Fair Havens, nor did they want to seek quarters for themselves and their passengers in the small town of Lasea. They knew the ship could not reach Italy at this point. Their discussion involved whether the ship should move to a better harbor along the same coast. They knew of another harbor a little to the west on Crete named Phoenix. It faced northwest and southwest, offering better shelter from the winds. The centurion agreed with the pilot and the ship's owner that wintering at this harbor would be best.

2. Facing a Storm (Acts 27:13-20)

When a gentle south wind began to blow, the sailors decided that conditions favored the short journey to Phoenix. The boat set off for this one-day cruise, carefully hugging the coast. As soon as they rounded Cape Matala and entered the gulf, six miles west of Fair Havens, a violent wind rushed down from the mountains of the island to the northeast striking the ship broadside. The sailors had not planned on this sudden change in the wind. Luke described this wind as one "of hurricane force" (27:14), a whirling, rotating wind formed by the clash of opposing air masses. More specifically, he called the storm the "northeaster," the deadly winter storm of the Mediterranean. The Alexandrian ship could not hold its course for Phoenix. The sailors had no option but to let the boat run with the wind away from land.

The wind carried the ship about 25 miles southeast to a small island called Cauda. When the ship came under the southern, sheltered (lee) side of Cauda, which offered some protection from the violence of the northeast winds, the sailors had the opportunity to take some measures to secure the vessel. With great difficulty they hauled aboard the lifeboat, the small boat normally towed behind the ship. During storms the danger existed of the lifeboat being swamped or dashed against the larger vessel. The lifeboat probably already had filled with water and become excessively heavy. Then the sailors passed ropes under the ship itself to hold it together. Finally, they lowered the sea anchor from the stern to drag in the water and slow their progress. The word translated "sea anchor" (27:17) could refer to the gear for the topsails, meaning they set only the small storm sail, allowing the ship to drift. In either case, the sailors acted on their fear of running aground on the sandbars of Syrtis in the shallow waters off the North African coast. Although this area was still about 400 miles distant, the sailors were taking no chances.

Verse 18: *We took such a violent battering from the storm that the next day they began to throw the cargo overboard.*

The measures the sailors took to secure the ship seemed inadequate as the *storm* continued to batter the ship. An ancient vessel could do little to fight such a fierce storm. The crew evidently had the mainsail down, allowing the wind to drive the vessel at its whim. By this time they probably were taking water on board as the ship dipped beneath the large waves, so the sailors began to lighten the ship's load by throwing *cargo overboard.* Perhaps they ejected any cargo stored on deck first.

Verse 19: *On the third day, they threw the ship's tackle overboard with their own hands.*

The situation became so desperate that *on the third day* the crew had to threw the *ship's tackle* overboard. This probably referred to spare gear or perhaps the ship's main yard, the long spar used to support the mainsail. On board the grain vessel the task would have required the combined manual effort of the crew.

Verse 20: *When neither sun nor stars appeared for many days and the storm continued raging, we finally gave up all hope of being saved.*

The storm clouds and heavy rain blotted out the *sun* by day and the *stars* by night *for many days.* With the stars hidden, the sailors had no way to locate their position since they had no compass in those days. The crew had no idea where they were in relation to land, rocks, or shoals. As the storm continued, the ship no doubt continued to leak. Since the sailors did not know the direction of the nearest land where they could run their ship ashore, the only recourse for a sinking ship, they were convinced they would sink. Humanly speaking, they appeared to have no chance of survival. Consequently, they *finally gave up all hope* of ever reaching safety and *being saved.* Other ancient sea stories also spoke of giving up all hope in the midst of a storm, but Luke described it in a special way, saying they *gave up hope of being saved.* Though he referred to physical salvation from death at sea, *saved* did have special Christian meaning, the spiritual salvation of the individual. Perhaps Luke intended some symbolic meaning. The word *saved* recalled that the One who would finally save the seafarers was the One who brings ultimate salvation and life.

Many of us depend on our own efforts to get us through crises only to find ourselves in seemingly hopeless situations. When we turn our eyes from ourselves and our crises to the Lord, we gain a new perspective of hope. We also find in the Lord an ever-present help in trouble and the strength to cope.

3. Encouraging Words (Acts 27:21-26)

Verse 21: *After the men had gone a long time without food, Paul stood up before them and said: "Men, you should have taken my advice not to sail from Crete; then you would have spared yourselves this damage and loss.*

Because of the disruption of the furious storm, those on board **had gone a long time without food.** Luke would take this point up in greater detail later (27:33). This showed the desperate straits in which the crew and passengers found themselves. They might have had little food available as a result of the storm's turbulence, or the people might have felt too sick or too dejected to eat. In the midst of this general dejection and despair **Paul stood up before them.** He could not resist the temptation to say in effect *I told you so.* The people in charge had rejected his good **advice** given at Fair Havens **not to sail from Crete.** They would have avoided all their suffering, damage to the vessel, and loss of cargo if the ship had stayed there. Paul's words of reminder were given to introduce a message of hope in the midst of despair. As his previous opinion had proved right, so he wanted them to take his next words with more confidence.

Verse 22: *But now I urge you to keep up your courage, because not one of you will be lost; only the ship will be destroyed.*

Paul gave his fellow shipmates what they most needed to hear, a message of encouragement and hope. He urged them to **keep up** their **courage** and not give in to despair. The apostle had warned them that loss of life, as well as the ship and cargo, would result from their setting sail from the port of Fair Havens. Now he qualified these earlier words with the assurance that **not one** of them would be **lost.** Although no person would lose his life, the **ship** would **be destroyed.**

Verse 23: *Last night an angel of the God whose I am and whom I serve stood beside me*

On the earlier occasion Paul apparently had offered his advice as an experienced sea traveler of sound judgment. Here the basis for his assurance of their deliverance was a divine revelation. The previous night an **angel** of **God** had appeared to him. This supernatural revelation produced his new confidence. The apostle described *God* as the One he served and to whom he belonged.

Verse 24: *and said, 'Do not be afraid, Paul. You must stand trial before*

Caesar; and God has graciously given you the lives of all who sail with you.'

The angel's message of comfort for this time of crisis contained two promises. After exhorting Paul *not* to *be afraid,* he first promised that the apostle *must stand trial before Caesar.* This confirmed the earlier revelation that Paul would reach Rome. God planned that Paul should witness there in the presence of the emperor (23:11). God's purpose would not fail. Second, the angel promised that God had *graciously given* him *the lives of all* those who were sailing with him. God not only would preserve Paul for his Roman witness but also would deliver all aboard the ship. In other words, Paul's presence on the ship guaranteed the deliverance of all the voyagers. Luke's wording implied that Paul had prayed for his fellow travelers and that God had heard and answered his prayer.

Verse 25: *So keep up your courage, men, for I have faith in God that it will happen just as he told me.*

On the basis of this divine revelation, Paul encouraged the *men* to *keep up* their *courage.* The apostle had faith in God. He believed that the Lord would fulfill His promise given through the angel. In effect, Paul wanted his fellow shipmates to share his faith that what God had promised to him would come to pass.

Verse 26: *Nevertheless, we must run aground on some island."*

The apostle warned the crew and passengers that even though God would deliver their lives, the ship itself would *run aground on some island.* They would all be cast ashore on this island, the identity of which had not been part of the angel's message.

Encouraging others to trust God can bring hope to them in the midst of difficult circumstances. We can remind ourselves and others that God is in control. He invites us to cast our anxieties on Him because He cares for us and will deliver us (1 Pet. 5:7).

4. Surviving Shipwreck (Acts 27:27-44)

Luke described the ship as being driven across the Adriatic Sea (27:27). This is not the modern Adriatic Sea that borders western Italy. In Luke's day the Adriatic Sea referred to the Ionian Sea and the north-central Mediterranean between Greece and Italy. For 14 days the storm had blown the ship westward the 475 miles from Cauda to Malta. During the 14th night after leaving Crete, the sailors sensed about midnight that they were approaching land. Perhaps the running swell of surf coupled with the noise of breakers alerted them to this possibility.

The crew began to take soundings. The first showed a depth of 120 feet and the second, 90 feet. The increasingly shallow water and the sound of breakers demanded safety measures. So the sailors let down four anchors, quite light in weight by modern standards. These would keep the ship from being wrecked against the rocks on an unknown coast in the darkness. The crew threw them off the stern to keep the vessel pointed toward the shore, allowing immediate control of the ship for beaching. The pagan sailors prayed to their gods for daylight to come.

The sailors planned their escape from the ship. In their scheme to save themselves they lowered the lifeboat into the sea, pretending that they were going to lower some anchors from the bow of the ship to give the ship more stability. The crew would have needed to set these out some distance from the bow, requiring use of the lifeboat. Somehow Paul understood the true motives of these men and reported the matter to Julius and his soldiers. The apostle knew to try to make shore in the morning without a full crew would lead to disaster. The rescue operation required their expertise. So Paul warned Julius that all would be lost if the sailors deserted the ship. Though the centurion had not listened to Paul earlier at Fair Havens, Julius took his advice here. The apostle had gained the centurion's respect. He ordered his men to cut the lines holding the lifeboat and let it fall away.

Verse 33: *Just before dawn Paul urged them all to eat. "For the last fourteen days," he said, "you have been in constant suspense and have gone without food—you haven't eaten anything.*

In this time of crisis Paul's leadership ability became even more evident. As day began to *dawn,* the apostle *urged all* the people on board *to eat.* He reminded the ship's company that they had not eaten since the terrible storm began *fourteen days* previously. The *constant suspense* of the dangerous threat to their lives weakened their appetites and made food preparation impossible. *Suspense* translates a word that means to wait with anticipation of either hope or fear. The situation had now improved. Paul was thinking in practical terms. The passengers and crew would need all the physical energy they could gather to make it safely to land.

Why did Paul, a prisoner, occupy such a leading position on the ship that he could command the attention of the people? In critical circumstances, they would hold a holy man, such as Paul, in higher regard than an ordinary person.

Verse 34: *Now I urge you to take some food. You need it to survive. Not one of you will lose a single hair from his head."*

Paul urged his shipmates *to take some food.* He told them they would *need it to survive.* Literally, the apostle said: *This is for your salvation.* Perhaps Paul was using this word to stress that the same God who delivered the voyagers from physical harm was the God who in Christ would give them ultimate salvation and true eternal life. In practical terms Paul knew that, by taking nourishment, the people on board would be prepared for the hard work of getting to shore. Food would give them fresh energy and enthusiasm for what had yet to be done. Paul assured them again that no harm would befall any of them. He used a biblical phrase to emphasize this: No one would *lose a single hair from his head* (see 1 Sam. 14:45). This proverb spoke of their preservation from danger.

Verse 35: *After he said this, he took some bread and gave thanks to God in front of them all. Then he broke it and began to eat.*

Paul encouraged those on the ship by example as well as by word. He first *gave thanks to God in front of them all* and *began to eat* bread. The breaking of bread and giving of thanks followed the normal Jewish and Christian practice of blessing a meal. Luke's description recalled that of the procedure Jesus used when feeding the multitudes (Luke 9:16) and when celebrating the Last Supper (Luke 22:19). Some Bible interpreters view the incident described in 27:35 as a celebration of the Lord's Supper. The fact that the meal was for a mixed company of people, mostly unbelievers, refutes that idea. Paul simply was observing his normal practice at a meal.

Verse 36: *They were all encouraged and ate some food themselves.*

Paul's example had the desired effect on the others. It *encouraged* them and they all *ate some food themselves.* Paul's own faith continued to serve as the source of their courage.

Luke added that 276 persons were aboard ship. Perhaps the count was made as part of the preparation for distributing the food. Luke might have helped in this activity and remembered the number. This detail further emphasized the Lord's providence and care in delivering this large number of people from the sea. Not one person suffered the least harm.

Strengthened by the food, the crew threw the cargo of grain overboard. This lightened the ship for running as far up on the beach as possible. Though they had thrown some of it overboard earlier, they would have had to keep some as ballast to provide stability while the ship was being driven by the wind.

When daylight came, the crew and passengers sighted land. The sailors did not recognize it and had no idea where they were. They did, however, see a bay with a sandy beach, a suitable spot to attempt to ground the vessel. Today the traditional site for Paul's shipwreck is known as St. Paul's Bay on the island of Malta. The sailors prepared to beach the ship by cutting the four stern anchors free. They also unlashed the ropes that had fastened the two steering paddles for safety during the storm, lowering them back into the water. Then they raised the small foresail so they could guide the ship toward the beach. The ship moved toward the beach, but some distance from the shore it ran aground on a sandbar with deep water on either side. The bow stuck fast and initially remained intact, but the pounding waves broke up the stern.

In the confusion the soldiers wanted to kill the prisoners to prevent them from escaping. Those able to swim could easily get ashore and take off into the countryside, making recapture difficult. Roman military law decreed that a guard who allowed his prisoner to escape was subject to the same penalty the escaped prisoner would have suffered. Julius, however, determined to protect Paul, prevented this action. Whatever the centurion's attitude toward his other prisoners, he did not want to put Paul's life in danger, especially in view of the apostle's help during the voyage. So Paul again provided the occasion of safety for his fellow passengers, in this instance the other prisoners. Also once again a Roman official intervened to save the life of the apostle. Julius gave the order that the men should make their way to land as best they could. He ordered those who could swim to jump in first. The rest made it to shore on planks or pieces from the ship's wreckage.

Verse 44b: *In this way everyone reached land in safety.*

Whether by swimming or using wreckage, ***everyone reached*** the shore safely. God in His providence delivered them all, as He had promised Paul. Indeed, the promise found fulfillment to the letter. The ship and cargo were lost, but every life on board was saved. Luke made clear that Paul's presence on the ship and God's protection of him led to the deliverance of all on board. Unlike Jonah, the apostle's presence was in no sense responsible for the storm. Had Julius and the captain followed Paul's advice, the ship would never have encountered the storm in the first place.

Crises may provide excellent opportunities to show and to share our faith in the Lord. God often chooses to use those of us who have faith in Him to encourage others to trust Him during extremely hard times. We can trust God's promises and testify to others about His faithfulness and His help in times past.

FOR FURTHER STUDY

1. See the map "Paul's Voyage to Rome" in *The Holman Bible Atlas,* page 256.

2. Read the article "Early Mediterranean Shipping" in the Spring 1995 issue of *Biblical Illustrator.*

3. Read the article "Crete" in the Spring 1989 issue of *Biblical Illustrator.*

4. See the articles "A Northeaster" and "Aristarchus" in the Winter 2000 issue of *Biblical Illustrator.*

The Week of February 25

WITNESSING TO THE WORLD

Background Passage: Acts 28:1-31
Lesson Passages: Acts 28:16-17a,22-28,30-31

INTRODUCTION

During a special outreach emphasis, our pastor encouraged us to pray daily for someone who was not a Christian. During a sermon he led us to mark key passages in a New Testament and then asked us to give that marked copy to the person for whom we had been praying. I gave my copy to a neighbor. Since that time, we have had several meaningful conversations about spiritual matters. She has told me that she has accepted Jesus Christ as her Lord and Savior. The Lord knows her heart; I continue to pray for her and have invited her to church. Although she has yet to visit, from time to time she calls me with questions about the Bible. Her openness to spiritual matters has given me an opportunity to witness.

This lesson focuses on Paul's witnessing during his house arrest in Rome. It emphasizes the apostle's witness to his own people as well as to Gentiles. It challenges us to use our witnessing opportunities.

Acts 28:1-31
1. Experiences on Malta (28:1-10)
2. Traveling to Rome (28:11-16)
3. Witnessing to the Jews (28:17-28)
4. Witnessing to All (28:30-31)

THE BACKGROUND

While in Ephesus on his third missionary journey, Paul had declared his desire to visit Rome, the capital and center of the empire (19:21). The Lord later promised him that he would testify in Rome (23:11). At last the apostle's desire and God's promise found fulfillment as he reached the great city. Under God's inspiration, Luke did not comment on two areas of interest in this account of Paul's activity in Rome. He did not relate the result of the apostle's appeal to Caesar, nor did he speak of his relationship with the Christian church that already existed in Rome. Instead, the focus is on Paul's encounter with the Jewish community in Rome.

The last chapter of Acts describes Paul's situation in Rome. He lived in his own rented house under military guard (28:16,30). Verses 16 and 30 frame two scenes involving the apostle's testimony to the Jews of Rome—an initial positive encounter (28:17-22) followed by a second meeting in which the Jews rejected Paul's message, at which point Paul concentrated his witnessing on the Gentiles (28:23-28).

The apostle had summoned the Jewish leaders to meet with him. He explained briefly how he came to be in Rome as a result of Jewish charges brought against him in Judea. This gave him the opportunity to explain to them the nature of the Christian message. First, the Jews listened to him. Then they resisted, resulting in Paul's turning to the Gentiles. The Jewish rejection of the gospel and its acceptance by Gentiles continues a major theme of Acts. The book ends with Paul in Rome, preaching Christ "boldly and without hindrance" to all who came to visit him while he was a prisoner (28:31).

THE LESSON PASSAGE

1. Experiences on Malta (Acts 28:1-10)

After their safe arrival on land, Paul and the shipwrecked party learned from local inhabitants that they had landed on the island of Malta, which lies 58 miles south of Sicily.

In God's providence He had delivered passengers and sailors practically on course to Italy, their initial destination. The word translated "islanders" (28:2) literally is "barbarians," which simply meant they did not know the Greek language. The Greeks and Romans thought strange languages sounded like nonsense syllables such as "bar-bar-bar," hence the word "barbarian." The shipwrecked party might have expected to be viewed by the islanders with suspicion and hostility. Yet the people of Malta showed the stressed travelers unusual kindness by welcoming them and building a fire to warm them from the rain and cold of the storm.

Paul had shown himself a practical, helpful person on board ship. He continued to make himself useful on land by gathering wood for the fire. In the bundle of sticks he was carrying was a snake. When he tried to cast the wood on the fire, the viper struck the apostle and fixed itself to his hand. Luke used a term that generally denoted a poisonous snake. Though no poisonous snakes live on Malta today, this does not reflect first-century conditions. The islanders obviously knew the snake as poisonous and expected Paul to die. They concluded that the apostle was a murderer whom justice had at last caught up with since he had not died at sea. Paul, however, merely shook the creature off.

The islanders continued to watch Paul, fully expecting the bite to result in some swelling or death. They waited in vain, for nothing happened.

They decided that instead of a fugitive Paul must be a god. Luke did not indicate whether Paul rebuked the islanders as he had done at Lystra when the people had hailed Paul and Barnabas as gods (14:15-18). Evidently no attempt was made to worship Paul on Malta. This incident emphasizes again how God completely protected Paul. Whether from a storm at sea or a snake on land, God miraculously rescued the apostle against all expectations. Both acts showed that God's purposes cannot be defeated.

The shipwrecked party landed near an estate belonging to the Roman governor of Malta, described as Publius, "the chief official of the island." As an act of official courtesy, Publius brought the survivors to his estate and entertained them for three days. Luke did not clarify who the "us" included. The welcome might have included only the Christian group and not the entire 276 from the ship. At least it included Paul and Luke.

The governor's father was sick, suffering from fever and dysentery. This might have been Malta fever, a sort of gastric illness caused by a microbe in goat's milk, common in Malta, Gibraltar, and other Mediterranean areas. Cases of Malta fever lasted an average of four months but in some instances as long as two or three years. The Lord healed Publius's father as Paul laid his hands on him and prayed for him. Word of the healing soon reached the surrounding areas, and the rest of the sick on the island came to Paul and were healed.

Paul's healing ministry led the people of the island to express their gratitude and appreciation by presenting him and his friends with gifts. When the three winter months were over and the ship's party was ready to continue their voyage, the people furnished them with the food and provisions needed for the rest of their journey.

2. Traveling to Rome (Acts 28:11-16)

Travel on the Mediterranean could not take place during the winter. Paul and his associates spent these three months on Malta, waiting for the favorable spring breezes. The beginning of winter also had forced other ships to lay over before completing their journeys. The centurion, Julius, arranged for such a ship to take his group of prisoners and soldiers on to Italy. Paul and his colleagues boarded an Alexandrian vessel, probably another grain ship from Egypt. Luke reported that the ship's figurehead bore the images of the twin gods, Castor and Pollux, the sons of Zeus and Leda. The constellation Gemini represented these gods. Sailors considered viewing this constellation a sign of smooth sailing.

The ship sailed first to Syracuse, the chief city of Sicily. Syracuse was about 90 miles from Malta and located on the eastern extremity of southern Sicily. The vessel remained there for three days, perhaps waiting for better wind conditions as well as loading and unloading cargo. From

Syracuse the ship sailed to Rhegium, an important harbor at the southern tip of the boot of Italy, just opposite Sicily and at the entrance to the straits of Messina, a voyage of about 70 miles. It docked there to await a more favorable breeze. On the next day a south wind began to blow, and the ship sailed approximately 200 miles up the coast of Italy to Puteoli in only two days. Puteoli was a resort city on the bay of Naples and the principal port for the grain ships from Egypt. It was about 130 miles from Rome.

At Puteoli Paul and his companions found some Christians who invited the group to spend a week with them. That Paul found believers in Puteoli is not surprising, for it was an important city whose population included a colony of Jews. That Paul, a prisoner, was allowed to seek out these Christians and spend seven days in fellowship with them is surprising. Julius trusted Paul and granted him unusual privileges. Luke did not mention the centurion and the soldiers after chapter 27.

The route from Puteoli to Rome took about five days by foot. Before Paul reached the city, he received a welcome from two groups of Christians sent out to meet him and escort him back to Rome. Evidently the Christians at Puteoli sent word to those in Rome immediately on Paul's arrival in Puteoli. One group got as far as the Forum of Appius, 43 miles south of Rome, and the other got only as far as Three Taverns, 33 miles from Rome. These were well-known stopping places on the Via Appius that led from Rome through Puteoli to the south of Italy. Paul thanked God for these believers.

Luke only mentioned the Roman Christians at this point in Acts. Their presence assured the support and encouragement of the Christian community for the apostle's witness in the city.

Verse 16: *When we got to Rome, Paul was allowed to live by himself, with a soldier to guard him.*

Paul at last arrived at his destination. With his arrival Luke closed the long travel narrative and opened the account of Paul's witness in Rome. He also ended the last "we" section in Acts. At Rome Paul *was allowed to live by himself* in private quarters with only a single *soldier* to guard him at all times. This showed that the apostle had considerable liberty though still under Roman custody. This arrangement enabled him to bear his Christian witness. Luke and Aristarchus must have remained with Paul through most, if not all, of his house arrest at Rome. From time to time such friends as Epaphras, John Mark, Demas, and Jesus who was surnamed Justus joined them (Col. 4:10-14; Philem. 23-24).

3. Witnessing to the Jews (Acts 28:17-28)

Verse 17a: *Three days later he called together the leaders of the Jews.*

Paul took *three days* to settle into his new residence. He then *called together* the Jewish *leader*s of Rome to meet with him in his own rented quarters. He invited them to come to him since he was officially confined to the house.

Rome had an extensive Jewish community consisting of a number of separate synagogues. The leaders of the Jewish community with whom Paul met were probably the ruling elders of these various Roman synagogues. Perhaps Paul wanted to learn what they had heard from Jerusalem about him and to find out their attitude toward him. Primarily, though, he hoped the occasion would give him an opportunity to proclaim the message about Jesus, the Messiah.

In 28:17 Paul began with the formal term of address used at Jewish gatherings, "My brothers," meaning fellow Jews. He informed the leaders of the reasons he was in Rome. His words sum up his defenses recorded in chapters 22—26 and emphasize Paul's total innocence. He pointed out that he had "done nothing against" the Jewish "people" or the "customs" of their "ancestors." The Asian Jews in Jerusalem had made those precise charges against the apostle. Paul, however, truthfully pointed out that the Jewish charges were false and that he had been a law-abiding Jew in every sense. Saying the Jews "arrested" him in "Jerusalem" and handed him "over to the Romans" summarized the scene in the temple where the Romans intervened to rescue Paul from the angry Jewish mob, placing him under arrest.

The Romans had examined Paul. They found he had done nothing that deserved death and therefore he should have been acquitted and set free. Paul's statement again summarized the account of events. Though the Romans wanted to release him as far as the facts of his case were concerned, Jewish pressure led the Roman governors to keep him confined. Paul explained to the Roman Jews that he had to appeal to Caesar because the Jerusalem Jews objected to the Roman desire to set Paul free.

In 28:19 Paul made clear that he was not attacking the Jewish nation for the way its leaders had acted. He had no charge to make against his own people. He was not guilty of any crime against the Jews, nor was he guilty of any ill intent toward them. Though they had falsely accused him, he would make no accusations against them.

Paul emphasized that he had called the Roman Jews together to inform them about his situation. The real point of disagreement between him and his accusers at Jerusalem had to do with the messianic hope of Israel. Paul believed Jesus of Nazareth and His resurrection fulfilled this hope; they did not. For the hope of Israel Paul found himself in chains (28:20).

The answer of the Roman Jewish leaders to Paul, though surprising, was a model of diplomacy. They professed complete ignorance about the apostle and his case, stating that they had received no official letters from

Judea or even an oral report about Paul. In light of the regular communication between Rome and the East, these Roman Jews should have had some idea of the trouble that had arisen over Paul. Perhaps due to winter travel conditions, no one from the holy land had arrived in Rome before Paul. On the other hand, the leaders of the Sanhedrin in Jerusalem may have realized that, if they could not successfully prosecute Paul before provincial rulers, they had even less chance of doing so against a Roman citizen in Rome before Caesar. Another possibility is that the Roman Jews knew more than they claimed but wanted to distance themselves from Paul and the Christian faith. They had not forgotten that earlier disputes and riot over the Messiah in their community had led to their temporary expulsion from the city by the emperor Claudius in A.D. 49 or 50.

Verse 22: *But we want to hear what your views are, for we know that people everywhere are talking against this sect."*

The Roman Jews implied that their knowledge of the Christian faith came only from hearsay—*people everywhere are talking against this sect.* The English word *heresy* comes from the Greek term translated *sect.*

The Jewish claim again seems much too diplomatic. They had to know something of the Christian faith because an active Christian church existed in Rome. Paul had written a letter to the church there, and Roman Christian brothers had met Paul on his way to Rome (28:15). The Roman Jews presumably had heard of Paul and his reputation as a leading missionary. Regardless, however, these Jews were willing at a future time to hear Paul's *views* on this sect. They wanted to learn what he had to say for himself and to see why he was so out of favor with the Jewish authorities in Jerusalem.

Verse 23: *They arranged to meet Paul on a certain day, and came in even larger numbers to the place where he was staying. From morning till evening he explained and declared to them the kingdom of God and tried to convince them about Jesus from the Law of Moses and from the Prophets.*

The Jews **arranged** a second meeting with Paul, and this time an *even larger* group came to see the apostle. Luke noted that the meeting lasted *from morning till evening.* Paul did not talk about his own situation. Instead, he devoted the entire day to presenting the gospel as he would have done if he could have attended the synagogue. The terms **kingdom of God** and **Jesus** summarized the content of Paul's message (see also 28:31). The two concepts formed a unity. Jesus, as God's redemptive agent, the Messiah, stands at the center of God's sovereign rule. God's people gather around Him. The Jews looked for the coming of the Messiah and the restoring of God's kingdom in a renewed Israel. Paul preached that this already had occurred in Jesus.

Paul sought to **convince** the Jews through an exposition of the

Scriptures. *Convince* implied that he combined proclamation with persuasion and that the Jews and Paul debated the issues with emotion. The apostle based his argument on the **Law of Moses** and the **Prophets.** In Paul's discussions with Jews, the Old Testament Scriptures typically provided the main evidence. The debate centered on their interpretation and whether Jesus fulfilled the Old Testament prophecies. Luke did not provide the texts Paul used to expound Jesus. They probably pointed to the necessity of the Messiah's suffering and to His resurrection. Jesus Himself set those texts before the disciples after His resurrection (Luke 24:27,44-47). Paul had expounded those Scriptures in the synagogue of Pisidian Antioch (Acts 13:16-43).

Verse 24: *Some were convinced by what he said, but others would not believe.*

Paul's preaching resulted in the same kind of mixed response he had experienced on previous occasions. *Convinced* could mean merely that some of the Roman Jews found Paul's arguments persuasive rather than that they personally accepted Jesus as the Christ. Throughout Acts, however, we read that individual Jews did believe when **others would not believe.** The Jews as a whole, or the synagogue in an official sense, did not accept Paul's witness to Christ.

Verse 25: *They disagreed among themselves and began to leave after Paul had made this final statement: "The Holy Spirit spoke the truth to your forefathers when he said through Isaiah the prophet:*

The meeting broke up with the Jews arguing **among themselves.** Before they left, Paul got in one last word. He cited Scripture. The Old Testament prophecy did not apply to the Christ but rather to the Jews and their refusal to hear the word of God. The **Holy Spirit** had spoken about them through the words **Isaiah** originally had addressed to their **forefathers.** This emphasized the divine inspiration of the prophet's words. God's Spirit speaks through the written Word.

Paul began to separate himself from the unbelieving Jews. Earlier he had addressed them as *my brothers* (28:17). Here he spoke of **your** forefathers. Paul did not include himself with the hardhearted forefathers who had rejected God's word through Isaiah nor with their descendants who continued to resist the Spirit. Paul had not stopped being a Jew, but his faith in Christ sharply separated him from Jews who rejected the gospel.

Verse 26: " *'Go to this people and say,*
"You will be ever hearing but never understanding;
you will be ever seeing but never perceiving."

Paul quoted the text of Isaiah 6:9-10 from the Septuagint, the Greek translation of the Hebrew Scriptures. Jesus had quoted this text when He referred to the failure of the Jews to understand and appropriate the message of His parables (Luke 8:10). Paul also had used it earlier in writing to the Roman Christians (Rom. 11:8). The quote placed the entire blame for Israel's separation from God on their own stubbornness. The words highlighted the three organs of perception—the ears *(hearing),* the eyes *(seeing),* and the *heart* (28:27). Hebrews considered the heart the organ of understanding and will. Isaiah pictured people who merely took in sensory data without *understanding.* Their ears heard the sounds but did not comprehend. Their eyes took in the sights but without *perceiving.*

Verse 27: *For this people's heart has become calloused;*
> *they hardly hear with their ears,*
> *and they have closed their eyes.*
Otherwise they might see with their eyes,
> *hear with their ears,*
> *understand with their hearts*
and turn, and I would heal them.'

The people's lack of understanding resulted from their *calloused* or hardened *heart.* They did not want to see or hear God's truth, for they had no intention of obeying. If they had heard and understood His message, they would have turned from their ways in repentance and received God's healing. This indicated divine judgment on them because they had hardened their hearts against God. They did not want to change their ways.

God's Word defines and diagnoses sin. While we may find hearing and accepting the Word difficult, the Spirit uses the Word to wound in order to *heal.* When persons deliberately refuse the Word, their hearts become *calloused*—they eventually deprive themselves of the capacity to receive it.

Verse 28: *"Therefore I want you to know that God's salvation has been sent to the Gentiles, and they will listen!"*

Israel's hardened attitude toward the gospel resulted in the message of **God's salvation** being **sent** directly to the **Gentiles** who would respond positively: *they will listen!* The conference at Jerusalem (Acts 15) had affirmed that the gospel was for both Jews and Gentiles. On Paul's missionary travels he proclaimed the gospel first to Jews, then to Gentiles. He followed that same pattern at Rome.

The apostle had described his ministry as primarily to the Gentiles (Gal. 2:8). God's message to him in the temple had confirmed this (Acts 22:21). Throughout Acts Luke depicted Paul as having great success among the Gentiles. So in Rome the apostle also directed his efforts to the Gentiles. However, he never gave up on the Jews. His letters indicated that he looked for them to have a change of heart in due time. Yet for the moment his mission efforts turned to the Gentiles.

Some ancient manuscripts include after verse 28 the words "After he said this, the Jews left, arguing vigorously among themselves," so some translations include these words as verse 29. The manuscripts Bible students consider more reliable, however, do not include those words. For this reason the *New International Version* omits verse 29 from the text, making it a footnote or marginal notation.

Paul created a witnessing opportunity by inviting the Jewish leaders to his house. We should do what we can to create our own opportunities to witness, especially when circumstances limit our outreach. While we should not ignore individuals or groups who are hardened to the gospel, we may target our witness to those who will listen and perhaps respond positively. Prayer will help us discern both how to create witnessing opportunities and whom we should target.

4. Witnessing to All (Acts 28:30-31)

Verse 30: *For two whole years Paul stayed there in his own rented house and welcomed all who came to see him.*

For *two whole years* Paul continued to remain in *his own rented house.* Keeping a dwelling at his own expense implied that the apostle had some means of income. Prisoners could in certain circumstances carry on their own trades. Though Paul did not have the freedom to move about, he could still preach and serve as a missionary since people could come to *see him.* Paul graciously received *all* who came to visit him in his house. This probably included Jews as well as Gentiles. Acts strongly stresses the inclusive nature of the gospel. God's salvation has been offered to all human beings.

Verse 31: *Boldly and without hindrance he preached the kingdom of God and taught about the Lord Jesus Christ.*

The apostle preached **boldly and without hindrance** the **kingdom of God.** *Boldly* implies publicly, candidly, and forcefully. *Without hindrance* shows the tolerance of Rome at that time toward Christianity and the gospel proclaimed. The Romans put no obstacle in the way of Paul's testimony to the gospel since they did not view it as dangerous or rebellious. The apostle also **taught about the Lord Jesus Christ.** The good news of God's *kingdom* is the good news about *Christ*, the Door to the kingdom.

Luke closed his two-volume work on this victorious note. Despite all the difficulties and misunderstandings, the proclamation of the kingdom of God and of the Lord Jesus Christ moved forward through the Jewish homeland into the Roman Empire *without hindrance.* The gospel remained free, triumphant over every barrier of superstition and human prejudice. People could not stop its progress and ultimate victory. The gospel had triumphed, but Paul remained in chains, a prisoner. Throughout Acts people rejected, beat, reviled, imprisoned, and killed those who proclaimed the gospel; but the good news remained unchained and victorious.

Luke's ending does not satisfy most readers. What happened to Paul?

Luke gave no details about the apostle's two years in Rome. Some Bible students believe Luke ended Acts at this point because he wrote it during Paul's imprisonment and did not know what would happen next. Perhaps he hoped to write a third volume, taking up the story from this point. That view, however, requires a very early date for Acts.

Some students believe that the Romans executed Paul at the end of his two-year house arrest and that Luke did not speak of his death because that would have ruined his portrayal of the triumphant advance of the gospel. Others assume that Paul's case never came to trial because the prosecutors failed to appear within the period of statutory limitations in Roman law. Luke expected his readers to understand that if Paul did not appear before Caesar within this period he would have been set free. But during the storm at sea, the angel of the Lord had assured Paul that he would stand trial before Caesar (27:24).

All these positions have pros and cons; none can be proved conclusively. Perhaps we should understand that Luke simply ended Acts at this point because the Spirit had accomplished His purpose. Paul was in Rome preaching the gospel without hindrance. Acts presented the advance of the gospel from Jerusalem toward "the ends of the earth" (Acts 1:8).

Whatever the outcome of Paul's Roman imprisonment, Luke was led of the Spirit to end the account where he did. He ended, not with the focus on Paul but on the gospel of Jesus Christ—the central focus of Acts. Based on information in Paul's Pastoral Letters, the Romans probably did release Paul from this imprisonment. He enjoyed a period of freedom and continued his evangelistic work. He was arrested again and eventually executed (2 Tim. 4:6-18).

When we commit to witness to others about Jesus, God will give us opportunities to follow through on our commitment. We now have the opportunity to witness to the world because the world has come to our country. Will we commit ourselves to proclaim Christ to the people in our individual worlds?

FOR FURTHER STUDY
1. Read "Paul: His Roman Ministry and Death" in the Summer 1979 issue of *Biblical Illustrator.*

2. Read "Rome" in the Summer 1987 issue of *Biblical Illustrator.*

3. Read "From Malta to Rome" in the Spring 1995 issue of *Biblical Illustrator.*

4. See the map "Paul's Voyage to Rome" in *The Holman Bible Atlas,* 256.